AMERICANS
MOVING TO CANAD

WELCOME TO CANADA

A WORD TO THE WISE

Don't forget to download e-book version of this book in pdf format to enjoy crisp clear color photos and active links.
So you can enjoy your reading on Ipod, PDA or on any hand held device. E-book is also low priced. Please check at www.ebookmall.com or any other e-book vender.

Always Be In A Good Position When The Puck Is Dropped

I'M SORRY, IDIOTS WINNING ELECTIONS IS NOT A GOOD ENOUGH REASON TO GRANT YOU POLITICAL ASYLUM...
AFTER ALL, WE'RE CANADIANS, YOU KNOW!
WANTED
YAY
NEIGH
PONSONBY BRITT
UM, ARE YOU SURE THE CANADIAN NATIONAL ANTHEM IS MAPLE LEAF RAG?
EH?
greg © 2004 08-11-04

AMERICANS MOVING TO CANADA

HOW TO MOVE & WHAT YOU NEED TO KNOW FOR STRESS FREE SETTLEMENT

WITH

YOUR TAX AND FINANCIAL PLANNING TIPS TO MAXIMIZE YOUR ASSETS

Editor

Tariq Nadeem

ISBN: 978-0-980-9203-4-5 (Paperback)

ISBN: 978-0-980-9203-5-2 (e-book)

This book is printed on acid free paper.

Send your wholesale inquiries in U.S.A to Ingram Book Group, Baker & Taylor, and Nacscorp.

In United Kingdom and Europe send your wholesale inquiries to Bertram and Blackwell's.

For retail purchase visit your local Amazon and Barns and Nobles online bookstores or checkout with your local bookstore.

For reprint/co-publishing rights contact Self-Help Publishers at info@selfhelppublishers.com or visit www.selfhelppublishers.com

Manufactured in United States of America and United Kingdom simultaneously by arrangements with Self-Help publishers.

Cover design and layout by Lisa Walter

Acknowledgement & Credits

Moving to Canada, Eh?Let Slate help you decide if it's really for you.
By Dahlia Lithwick and Alex Lithwick

Taxation in Canada
http://en.wikipedia.org/wiki/Taxation_in_Canada

Preface -Our $100 Trillion National Debt
By Biby Bill Walkerll

Disclaimer

Federal government of Canada and Provincial governments of Canada and their ministers, employees, agents , directors, author, editor shall not be liable for any losses, claims, demands, injuries, causes of action, actions, damages suffered by the user or users of this publication.

Portions of this book have been provided courtesy of Citizenship and Immigration Canada. The Government of Canada does not endorse or support any annotations or commentary included in this publication. These are the sole responsibility and choice of the author/editor.

Some of the Content in this publication may have been compiled from a variety of sources and is subject to change without notice. Although every effort has been made to contact the copyright holders of materials, if readers of this report consider materials to be their copyright and have not been contacted by the author, please contact the publisher.

Parental Advisory: Mature/Explicit Content

Displayed art and photos may feature scenes of a nature not intended for young readers/ viewers. (IE anyone under the age of 18) If you are underage please skip contents featured for mature reader/viewers audience.

CANADA

A Canadian Presence

DEDICATION

This book is dedicated to all those peace lovers
who wish to make Canada their homeland.

To those who encourage people to focus on productive outcomes that advance and unite civilization. To those with peaceful imagination that seek to minimize alienation and celebrate interdependence rather than self sufficiency, inclusion rather then exclusion, openness, opportunity and hope rather than limits, suspicion and grievance. To all those who act to keep and maintain peace on planet Earth.

"In order to rally people, governments need enemies. They want us to be afraid, to hate, so we will rally behind them. And if they do not have a real enemy, they will invent one in order to mobilize us.": **Thich Nhat Hanh** - Vietnamese monk, activist and writer.

"Though force can protect in emergency, only justice, fairness, consideration and cooperation can finally lead men to the dawn of eternal peace": **Dwight David Eisenhower** : 34th president of the United States, 1890-1969

"I am tired and sick of war. Its glory is all moonshine. It is only those who have neither fired a shot nor heard the shrieks and groans of the wounded who cry aloud for blood, more vengeance, more desolation. War is hell." - - **William Tecumseh Sherman**

"When good does evil in its struggle against evil, it becomes indistinguishable from its enemy."

T.S. Elliot

"The truth will set you free, but first it will make you miserable".
James Garfield 1831-1881, 20th U.S. President

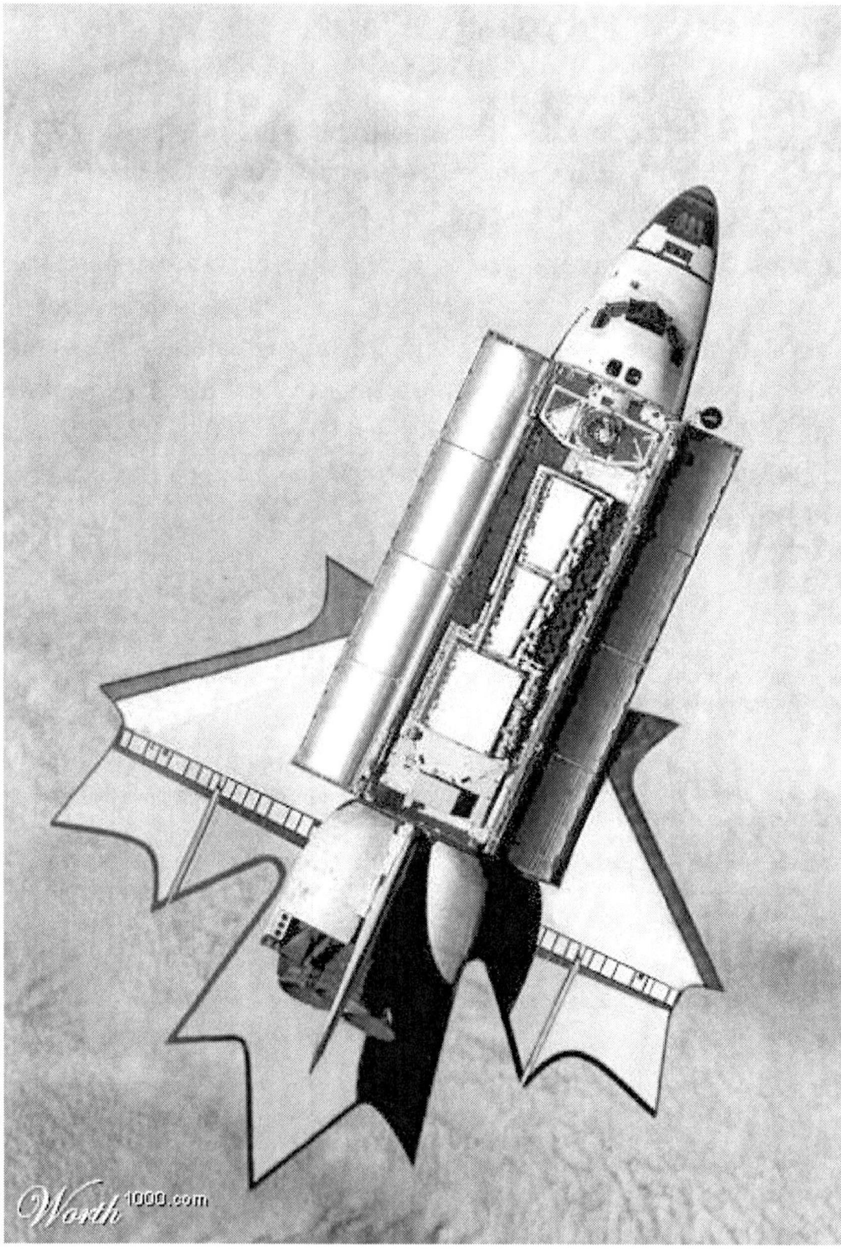
Worth1000.com

PREFACE

America's $100 Trillion National Debt

08/08/08 "Lew Rockwell" -- - The "official" debt of the United States is only around $10 trillion dollars as of August 6, 2008. This is a manageable number; we could pay it off in a few decades if we quit buying luxuries like food and clothing, and take a few other minor economy measures. Unfortunately, the "$10 trillion" number was produced by government accounting, which among other things allows one to ignore Social Security, Medicare, and the new prescription drug benefit. This is like ignoring rent, food, and utilities in your household budget... it will lead to a few bounced checks. Our real debt is about ten times higher.

Who says so? The President of the Dallas Federal Reserve, Richard W. Fisher. In a May speech at the Commonwealth Club of California, he states that the US national debt is close to $100 trillion. You can read his whole speech at the Federal Reserve web site.

The Real Debt

Here is what he said regarding the actual US debt:

"Add together the unfunded liabilities from Medicare and Social Security, and it comes to $99.2 trillion over the infinite horizon. Traditional Medicare composes about 69 percent, the new drug benefit roughly 17 percent and Social Security the remaining 14 percent."

Interested readers will notice that the new prescription drug benefit is projected to be more fiscally crushing than all of Social Security.

Mr. Fisher points out that this $99.2 trillion will be a bit of a burden to pay off:

"Let's say you and I and Bruce Ericson and every U.S. citizen who is alive today decided to fully address this unfunded liability through lump-sum payments from our own pocketbooks, so that all of us and all future generations could be secure in the knowledge that we and they would receive promised benefits in perpetuity. How much would we have to pay if we split the tab? Again, the math is painful. With a total population of 304 million, from infants to the elderly, the per-person payment to the federal treasury would come to $330,000. This comes to $1.3 million per family of four—over 25 times the average household's income."

You do have $1.3 million in your pocket, right? What, are you some kind of deadbeat?

Speaking of deadbeats, the "$99.2 trillion" estimate does not include the subprime bailout. So for those who like large round numbers, by the end of 2008 the real National Debt should be large, round, and about $100 trillion.

Other Unfunded Liabilities

The Fed's numbers do not include some other liabilities the US has acquired over the years. One massive but unquantifiable liability is the probability of future wars. If it cost the US hundreds of billions of dollars to invade the fifth-rate kleptocracy of Iraq and the foreign-aid regime of Afghanistan, how many trillions would wars against real powers cost? Perhaps I should ask "how many US cities" such wars would cost.

Some nations could legitimately plan for peace. Sweden has not fought a foreign war since 1814 (as many Swedes have pointed out in emails regarding my Swiss article). Switzerland, not since 1815. The US record is less hopeful.

The US is rarely *not* in foreign wars, and the current Administration has openly announced that the "Global War On Terror" will never end. Yet our government accounting is predicated on perpetual peace, on an ever-increasing flow of money into the official pyramid schemes.

In any case, whether you are pro- or anti- Empire, real accounting demands some reserves for future war contingencies. When even a few US cities are burning radioactive pyres, the flow of funds to Social Security and Medicare will suffer some interruption.

Any fiscal plan demands amortization of the accumulated hatred our foreign adventures have accumulated. The US taxpayer has aided every evil dictator since 1945. Stalin, Castro, Pol Pot, Nyerere, Idi Amin, go right down the roster and US money helped pay for the barbed wire and bullets (and the nuclear reactors, in the case of the Kim Dynasty rulers of Korea).

So far blowback has been quite mild. But in a world full of easy do-it-yourself WMD technologies, our luck can't hold forever. If the US were a private company, the "badwill" on our books would reach into the tens of trillions.

Tearing Up The Credit Cards

Most likely, the US will simply continue into bankruptcy. This is the most common pathway for nations with fiat currencies and unchecked ruling classes. But let's assume that somehow a Clone Army of 435 Ron Pauls gets into Congress, while genetic technology brings back Jefferson and Gallatin to their old offices. Can the US be made solvent again?

I think so. Most of the unfunded liability is medical. We know why the medical system does not work. So if we eliminate the FDA, guild restrictions on medical professions, and the ridiculous tax laws that force us into medical-insurance serfdom to employers, we could cut medical costs enough to phase out Medicare and the new "drug benefit." In this way more than half the shadow debt can be wiped out.

The answer for the Social-Security pyramid scheme is well known. Chile fixed its Social Security disaster decades ago, by giving large IRA-style allowances and phasing out the government payments to younger recipients. The sooner we do this the easier it will be… the Boomers start retiring soon.

Most important, we have to listen to the Founder's calls for free trade with all nations but entangling alliances with none. The US cannot stop every quarrel in the world even if we wished… and the actual record of our foreign-policy geniuses has been to send a couple of trillion dollars out to the very worst criminals in human history. Aid To Dependent Dictators must stop.

None of this will happen while Mordor-On-The-Potomac still possesses its plutonium credit card, the Fed. Just as we would for any other bankrupt relative, we must help Uncle Sam cut up his credit cards.

By Bill Walker:]He is a research technologist. He lives with his wife and four dogs in Grafton NH, where they are active in the Free State Project.

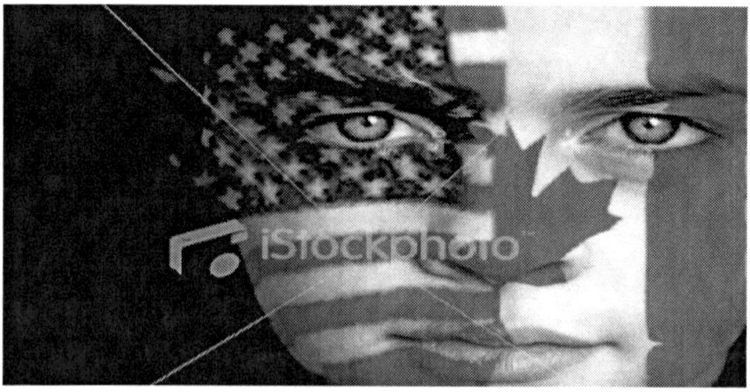

CONTENTS

Chapter 3

Chapter 4

Chapter 5

Chapter 6

Chapter 7

Chapter 8

Chapter 9

Chapter 10

Chapter 11

Chapter 12 Your Settlement Guide

GETTING READY -- BEFORE YOU LEAVE FOR CANADA-contents

Chapter 13 - THE DAY YOU ARRIVE IN CANADA-contents

Chapter 14 - YOUR FIRST FEW DAYS IN CANADA-contents

Chapter 15 - FINDING A JOB, BUILDING A FUTURE-contents

Chapter 16 - GENERAL INFORMATION ABOUT CANADA-contents

Chapter 17 - THE CANADIAN WAY OF LIFE-contents

Chapter 18 - STANDARDS AND EXPECTATIONS-contents

Chapter 19 - YOUR RIGHTS AND OBLIGATIONS-contents

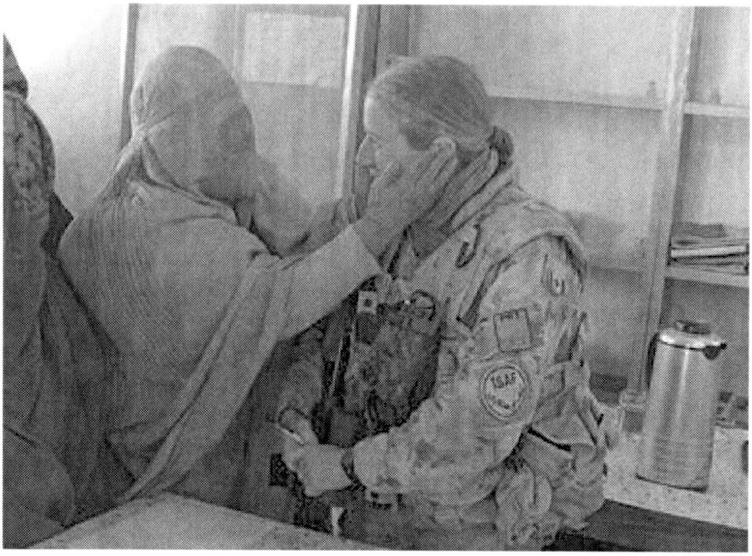

A Canadian Peacekeeping female soldier is greeted by an elderly Afghan women

Sir, can you please step out of your car? I pulled you over for failing to wave "thank you" at the station wagon who let you merge back there.

AIR CANADA
SURCLARO.COM

Chapter 1

Americans Really Are Moving to Canada

A recent analysis of immigration statistics by a Canadian firm showed the number of Americans who moved to Canada in 2006 hit a 30-year high.

An analysis of immigration statistics done by the Montreal-based Association for Canadian Studies showed the number of Americans who moved to Canada in 2006 hit a 30-year high, almost double the number who moved north in 2000 when Bush was elected for a first term as U.S. president.

The analysis also showed the southward brain drain is being narrowed somewhat, and most of the American migrants are highly educated people who may be moving to Canada for quality of life and social reasons.

The numbers were not huge – 10,942 Americans moved to Canada last year, far smaller than the influx predicted when bogus maps of the United States of Canada began hitting the Internet in the waning days of the 2004 campaign.

The day after Bush was re-elected president, there were 191,000 hits on Canada's immigration website, six times its average traffic, most of it from the U.S.

Websites sprouted explaining the mechanics of the Canadian immigration system, and Canadian women, tongues in cheek, offered to marry anti-war Americans.

But the increase is symbolic, said Jack Jedwab, the executive director of the association that analyzed the statistics. "Given that most of these immigrants are university-educated or better, you can assume they can find work in the U.S., so the move must be based on other reasons," Jedwab said.

Citizenship and Immigration Canada reported that 49.5 per cent of the Americans who migrated to Canada in 2006 had at least a bachelor's degree.

Jedwab said anecdotal information points to politics, health care, social issues, possibly even the strengthening Canadian dollar as lures northward, he said.

For 34-year-old labour organizer Tom Kertes, the move last April from Seattle, Wash., to Toronto was based on human rights.

"The words `human rights' are foreign words in the U.S.," Kertes said.

"They only apply to other countries."

He moved to Toronto with his partner Ron Braun and the two plan to marry, something they could not do in Washington state.

He also cited the war in Iraq and the torture of Iraqi prisoners by Americans – and the failure of the Bush administration to clearly disavow such practice – as contributing factors to what is a major decision.

"Moving countries is not done lightly," he says.

He said he found the tolerance of Toronto welcoming and he thought Canadians were proud of their reputation for tolerance.

The 2006 figure marks the first time there have been more than 10,000 American migrants to Canada since 1981 and was the highest number since 1977.

Between 1967-75, a period marked by draft dodgers fleeing the Vietnam War, there were at least 19,000 Americans who fled north each year.

While the number of Americans moving north jumped, the number of Canadians moving to the United States declined to 23,913 in 2006 from 29,930 in 2005.

The net loss to Canada of 12,971 was the smallest since 2003 and slightly more than half of the loss suffered by Canada as recently as 2001 when 24,089 more Canadians moved south than Americans moved north.

The two largest categories of U.S. immigrants were the family class and economic class and Jedwab says he believes the numbers will continue to rise because of the family class of immigration.

"Once you reach a certain critical mass, the family reunification numbers tend to keep the numbers increasing," he said.

There was a large jump in the number of American refugees in 2006, but those were largely Haitians who received refugee status in the United States then moved to Canada.

Ontario – particularly the GTA region – was the destination of more than half of the U.S. migrants, far outpacing British Columbia and Quebec, the second and third most popular destinations.

Perhaps the most surprising aspect of the study is the attention it has received in the United States where it was first reported by abcnews.com.

It has become a hit on the blogosphere where many Americans have reacted with venom to those who have left the country and some 80,000 persons voted on whether they would move to Canada within hours of the question being posted on an aol.com site.

"If every American who didn't like George W. Bush left the country, there would be no one here but illegal immigrants," one blogger wrote.

Canada, Perhaps?

Clearly, there are those who simply want to live where George W. Bush does not. But geography, social norms and politics favor Canada as the most obvious refuge for discontented Americans.

If American liberals choose to escape to Canada, they won't be the first group in history to do so. Between 1763 and 1865, thousands of blacks migrated to Canada to escape the shackles of slavery. Between 1965 and 1975, thousands of men, and--interestingly--even more women, moved to Canada to defy the Vietnam war. Despite popular assumption, many were not even draft dodgers and made the move based on their convictions alone. Canada has been kind to self-proclaimed American refugees, who assimilate quickly and easily, never standing out as a particular group. Since Sept. 11, Americans have increasingly been migrating to Canada and are now the number one immigrant group there. Whether the 2004 U.S. presidential election leads to more migration to Canada won't be known for at least six months, as applications start to get approved.

Why Canada?For starters, Canada is literally right next door. Few Americans would have to fly. English is an official language in Canada. And American products, styles, customs, trends and even TV shows are widely available.

Beyond the obvious, for American Liberals, Canada represents all that America could be, and should be. Canada.....

It Represents the Vision Liberals Have for the USA

Canada...

1)...is a peaceful nation with no enemies, good international relationships (including with Cuba), and is at minuscule risk for a terror attack.

2)...has no abortion laws whatsoever, abortion is legal, without restriction. But the rate of abortions in the country is relatively low.

3)...in many provinces, recognizes and fully accepts gay marriage as a legal institution, even for immigration purposes.

4)...has socialized medicine that Canadians report satisfaction with. No Canadian goes without health care.

5)...has no death penalty.

6)... has tough gun control laws, and, it just so happens, a murder rate about three times lower than that in U.S.

7)...has a general maternity leave of one year off for mothers, at 80 percent of their salary.

8)... has a more balanced education system, where schools in poor areas deliver the same quality of education as those in wealthy locales.

As if that weren't enough to warrant serious thoughts of relocation by Kerry supporters, Canada is also: Culturally rich, diverse and multilingual; The per capita rate of college-educated residents is about 30 percent higher than the U.S. rate; The economy and standard of living are good; And, perhaps the clincher is that, overall, even the most conservative citizens disapprove of George W. Bush.

So How Easy is it for Americans to Migrate to Canada? Actually, it's easier than immigrating into the United States. Why? Because Canada's immigration system works on a points basis. No one criteria is demanded, rather for those without refugee or asylee status, or without family ties, a certain number of points are given for categories such as education, experience, arranged employment, age, language and adaptability. A person generally needs to accumulate 67 points to gain "landed immigrant status," which is similar to permanent resident (green card) status in the States.

In many cases, binational gay couples with no hope of being allowed to stay together in the U.S. (Because one party is not a resident), have been accepted, together as landed immigrants in Canada, basically because they had a degree and good work experience. In the U.S., only at the genius and celebrity levels do education and experience alone qualify one for a green card.

What About Other Countries? Australia is certainly a beautiful place, and English is the spoken language, but its laws are not as liberal as Canada's. Abortion is legal, but gay marriage was recently outlawed, for example. New Zealand and the U.K. are monarchies operating with a parliament, and are even less interested in constitutional changes than Australia is. They are becoming more popular among Americans who want to relocate, but not necessarily for political reasons.

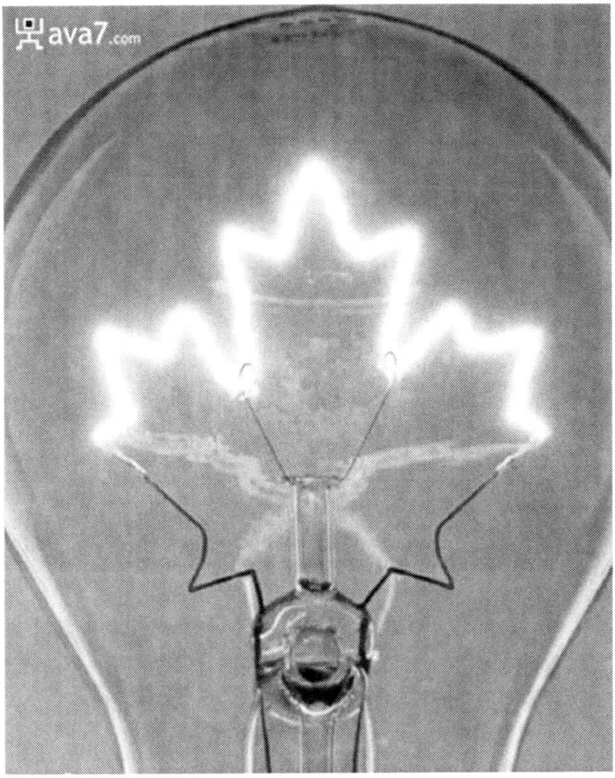

Some Americans, particularly those who are independently wealthy or ready to retire, consider non-English-speaking destinations as well. There's a growing contingent of American retirees to Mexico and the Caribbean. Switzerland is also increasingly popular with Yanks; the country has three official languages (German, French,

Italian) and a semiofficial language, Romanish (a mix of Roman and Latin), but English is spoken countrywide as well. As a conservative publication recently pointed out, Switzerland has the most democratic system in the world: Rather than voting for leaders who will make the laws, Swiss citizens vote on every issue up for consideration. Popular vote dictates law. This appeals more and more to the disheartened Democrat.

Dual-citizenship: But Will You Still be an American? In most countries, an immigrant can live, work and travel on a permanent resident card alone, which has no affect on citizenship status. However, citizenship has its benefits. If you want to naturalize in another country, can you stay American?

Be sure to check the local laws before making any decisions. They differ from country to country, and can change within countries from time to time. As of 2004, Canada, the U.K., Australia, New Zealand and Switzerland, as well as the United States government, all allow Americans to keep their U.S. citizenship even as they naturalize in a second country.

Before the disillusioned pack their bags and head for the border though, they might want to ask themselves how active they can be in American politics from afar. Are you one of the contemplators? If so, do you want to give up hope that your vision for America is a lost cause? Are you really ready to abandon ship? If so, well, some would say "Go for it." But then you might be able to migrate and still keep the faith too. After all, there's always the online campaign trail. And absentee ballots.

Moving to Canada, Eh? Let *Slate* help you decide if it's really for you.

One of the great frustrations of any Canadian is that well-intentioned Americans attempting to introduce other Americans to the *real* Canada seem to be in command of only about 12 words. Here they are in no particular order: loonies, toonies, snow, Tim Hortons, hockey, poutine, socialized medicine, DeGrassi Junior High, Pierre Elliott Trudeau, Labatt, French, and the expression "eh."

But there is *so* much more to Canada. Just ask any one of the many Canadians who are lurking about in your midst. (We lurk because we love.) There are great reasons, beyond frostbite and pink currency, to seriously consider relocation to the Great White. But still, Canada is still not for everyone. So here's a quiz, for those of you still considering joining the Bush-dodgers relocating to Canada. It isn't about loonies or toonies or socialized medicine. It's about the important stuff—stuff that will determine whether you really want to be a Canadian or just dress like one:

1) Do you like to shoot people? Circle one: yes / no

(If you answered "yes" you should know that there is no Second Amendment or equivalent thereof in the Canadian constitution. Perhaps as a consequence only 22 percent of Canadians own guns as opposed to 49 percent of Americans, while handguns and assault rifles are verboten. Perhaps related to that statistic, the violent crime rate in Canada is 10 times lower than in the United States. This may have no connection to guns, though, and rather a strong correlation to general mellowness of the Canadian temperament. (See Question 3, below.)

2) Have you recently shot someone? Circle one: yes / no

(If you answered yes, you may find Canada appealing. The Canadian courts abolished capital punishment in the '70s, and Canada hasn't seen an execution since 1962. Texas hasn't seen one since about 11 seconds ago.)

3) Do you like to smoke pot? Circle one: yes / no / only for medicinal reasons / only with John Ashcroft

(Judges in at least three provinces have now decriminalized marijuana possession and the federal government is considering decriminalizing it in small quantities. We are advised that the feds also grow great masses of it in large underground caverns and may soon expand the use of these caverns as shelters to which the entire country would retreat in the event of a terrorist attack or to spur mass-munchies in case of a national Doritos glut. And only in Canada would you find marijuana advocates genuinely arguing that people actually drive better stoned.)

4) Are you covered in vast quantities of coarse, black fur? Circle one: yes / no

(Don't kid yourself. It is freakin' cold up there. While 90 percent of Canadians live within 100 miles of the U.S. border, the places they live north of are Green Bay and Buffalo.)

5) Do you like to wear white sneakers (Canadians call these "running shoes") with jeans? Circle one: yes / no

(Canadians are an extraordinarily stylish people, without the excess snobbery of Europeans; and most of them manifest this by being strikingly well-shod. Canadians generally find themselves perplexed by shiny tracksuits, leggings, baseball caps, and sweaters with reindeer on them.)

6) Do you generally find being alive to be just fine? Circle one: yes / no

(For some reason Canadians seem to live longer, be healthier, and pay less for these privileges. It has something to do with national health insurance, adequate primary care, particularly for children, and the availability of quality prescription drugs. (See, e.g., Question 3, above.)

7) Are you gay, or, alternatively, do you suspect that the institution of marriage should be open to all couples who are committed to living together and/or raising children in a loving environment? Circle one: yes / no

(Six and possibly soon seven Canadian provinces currently permit gay marriage. Before leaving office last year, Prime Minister Jean Chretien referred the question of the constitutionality of same-sex marriage to the Supreme Court for an opinion. The court hasn't yet decided the question.)

8) Are your political views either too complicated to be expressed in two-word bumper stickers, or, alternatively, do you find that you just don't much care about your neighbors' views on guns/the unborn/or which deity is their copilot? Circle one: yes / no

(Canadians tend to subscribe to a live-and-let-live view of political ideology. It's not that Canadians don't care about their politics or moral issues. It's simply that they appear to operate under the assumption that, whatever their personal beliefs might be, you, their neighbor, may not care all that much to learn every detail of them on the way to the 7-Eleven. As a consequence, T-shirts in Canada are still funny, signage is still commercial, and bumpers are reserved for smashing into telephone poles after cottage parties. [Cottage: Def. Sprawling lakefront estate in rural Canada, quaintly Hamptonesque but with indoor plumbing optional.])

9) Are you bored to death of razor-thin margins between radical ideologues in every aspect of public life? Circle one: yes / no

(The 5-4 split on the Canadian Supreme Court is male/female as opposed to crazy/crazier.)

10) Does the idea of pluralism appeal to you? Not just in the sense that I-want-to-be-surrounded-by-lots-of-diverse-and-fascinating-people-who-all-worship-my-Lord, but rather, in the sense, that a country is a richer place for competing values, religions and cultures? Circle one: yes / no

(When Canadians talk about "multiculturalism," it doesn't only mean they're for blondes hanging out with redheads. Canadian TV shows actually teem with racially diverse characters, and the major national catalogs have been known to feature models in wheelchairs. Moreover, Canada has not one but two official languages, and no one seems to be suffering for it. Indeed, some believe it makes them sort of interesting. Certainly it will be interesting when the thousands of Bush-dodgers someday return to the United States to visit relatives and amuse them by explaining that the Teton Mountains actually mean "big boobies" in French.)

Worth 1000.com

2 Dollar Coin
"Toonie"

1 Dollar Coin
"Loonie"

50 Cent Coin

25 Cent Coin
"Quarter"

10 Cent Coin
"Dime"

5 Cent Coin
"Nickel"

1 Cent Coin
"Penny"

Chapter 2

Taxation in Canada

The level of **Taxation in Canada** is average among Organisation for Economic Co-operation and Development (OECD) countries. Approximately 70% of the Canadian government's income comes from taxation, the rest from tariffs, fees, and investments.[*citation needed*]

Administration

Federal taxes are collected by the Canada Revenue Agency (CRA), formerly known as "Revenue Canada" or the "Canada Customs and Revenue Agency".

Under "Tax Collection Agreements", CRA collects and remits to the provinces:

- Provincial personal income taxes on behalf of all provinces except Quebec, so that individuals outside of Quebec file only one set of tax forms each year for their federal and provincial income taxes.
- Corporate taxes on behalf of all provinces except Quebec, Alberta and Ontario.
- Provincial sales taxes in New Brunswick, Nova Scotia and Newfoundland and Labrador.

The *Ministère du revenu du Québec* collects the GST in Quebec on behalf of the federal government, and remits it to Ottawa.

History

When the Canadian federation was formed in 1867, the British North America Act attempted to create a federal government with unlimited revenue gathering abilities. The federal government was entrusted with the high cost programs of the time, most notably defence and the building of railways. The provinces were given limited taxation power as they could only impose direct taxes such as sales taxes, property taxes, and income taxes (although they also maintained control over most resource revenues as well). At the time, it was believed that the provinces had adequate revenue sources as major areas of provincial government spending today were generally not funded by the government (such as social assistance and medical care).

For the early part of Canadian history most federal government revenue came from tariffs on trade with excise taxes making up the rest of the government's funding. The largest source of provincial funding was licenses, permits, and transfers of funds from the federal government. The first corporate taxes were introduced at the end of the nineteenth century.

A crisis developed during the Great Depression because the provinces were responsible for skyrocketing welfare costs, but could not raise enough revenue since the taxes permitted to the provinces were so dependent on the health of the economy. The federal government still had considerable revenues however, which resulted in a system of transfer payments between the two levels of government. The transfer payments are still in place today.

The First World War had mostly been financed by traditional means, but in 1917, a tax on income was introduced as a temporary measure to fund the war. The income tax has since become a permanent feature of the Canadian tax system. The Second World War led to dramatic change in the tax system. The percentage of Canadian government revenue from indirect taxes fell from 90% in 1913 to less than 40% by 1946. Instead, Canadians began to pay income taxes and direct taxes has since provided the greatest bulk of government funding.

Income taxes

Personal income taxes

Both the federal and provincial governments have imposed income taxes on individuals, and these are the most significant sources of revenue for those levels of government accounting for over 40% of tax revenue. The federal government charges the bulk of income taxes with the provinces charging a somewhat lower percentage. Income taxes throughout Canada are progressive with the high income residents paying a higher percentage than the low income residents.

Where income is earned in the form of a capital gain, only half of the gain is included in income for tax purposes; the other half is not taxed.

Federal and provincial income tax rates are shown at Canada Revenue Agency's website.

Personal income tax can be deferred in a Registered Retirement Savings Plan (RRSP), a tax sheltered savings account or mutual fund that is intended to help individuals save for their retirement.

Corporate taxes

Companies and corporations pay tax on profit income and on capital. These make up a relatively small portion of total tax revenue. Tax is paid on corporate income at the corporate level before it is distributed to individual shareholders as dividends. A tax credit is provided to individuals who receive dividend to reflect the tax paid at the corporate level. This credit does not eliminate double taxation of this income completely, however, resulting in a higher level of tax on dividend income than other types of income. (Where income is earned in the form of a capital gain, only half of the gain is included in income for tax purposes; the other half is not taxed.) Corporations may deduct the cost of capital following capital cost allowance regulations.

Starting in 2002, several large companies converted into "income trusts" in order to reduce or eliminate their income tax payments, making the trust sector the fastest-growing in Canada as of 2005. Conversions were largely halted on October 31, 2006, when Finance Minister Jim Flaherty announced that new income trusts would be subject to a tax system similar to that of corporations, and that these rules would apply to existing income trusts after 2011.

Sales taxes

The federal government levies a multi-stage sales tax of 5% (6% prior to January 1, 2008), that is called the Goods and Services Tax (GST), and, in some provinces, the Harmonized Sales Tax (HST). The GST/HST is similar to a value-added tax.

All provincial governments except Alberta levy sales taxes as well. The provincial sales taxes of Nova Scotia, New Brunswick and Newfoundland and Labrador are harmonized with the GST. That is, a rate of 13% HST is charged instead of separate PST and GST. Both Quebec and Prince Edward Island apply provincial sales tax to the sum of price and GST. The territories of Nunavut, Yukon and Northwest Territories do not charge provincial sales tax.

Provincial and federal sales tax rates at the retail level on goods and some services are as follows:

- Alberta:..0 + 5% = 5%
- British Columbia:..........................7% + 5% = 12%
- Manitoba:.......................................7% + 5% = 12%
- Ontario:..8% + 5% = 13%
- Prince Edward Island:..10% + 5% = 15.5% (PST applied to price + GST)
- Quebec:..................... 7.5% + 5% = 12.875% (PST applied to price + GST)
- Saskatchewan:............5% + 5% = 10%

Property taxes

The municipal level of government is funded largely by property taxes on residential, industrial and commercial properties. These account for about ten percent of total taxation in Canada.

Excise taxes

Both the federal and provincial governments impose excise taxes on inelastic goods such as cigarettes, gasoline, alcohol, and for vehicle air conditioners. A great bulk of the retail price of cigarettes and alcohol are excise taxes. The vehicle air conditioner tax is currently set at $100 per air conditioning unit. Canada has some of the highest rates of taxes on cigarettes and alcohol in the world. These are sometimes referred to by Canadians as "sin taxes".

Payroll taxes

Ontario levies a payroll tax on employers, the "Employer Health Tax", of 1.95% of payroll. Eligible employers are exempt on the first $400,000 of payroll. This tax was designed to replace revenues lost when health insurance premiums, which were often paid by employers for their employees, were eliminated in 1989.

Quebec levies a similar tax called the "Health Services Fund". For those who are employees, the amount is paid by employers as part of payroll. For those who are not employees such as pensioners and self-employed individuals, the amount is paid by the taxpayer.

Premiums for the Employment Insurance system and the Canada Pension Plan are paid by employees and employers. Premiums for Workers' Compensation are paid by employers. These premiums account for 12% of government revenues. These premiums are not considered to be taxes because they create entitlements for employees to receive payments from the programs, unlike taxes, which are used to fund government activities. The funds collected by the Canada Pension Plan and by the Employment Insurance are in theory separated from the general fund. It should be noted that Unemployment Insurance was renamed to Employment Insurance to reflect the increased scope of the plan from its original intended purpose.

Employment Insurance is unlike private insurance because the individual's yearly income impacts the received benefit. Unlike private insurance, the benefits are treated as taxable earnings and if the individual had a mid to high income for the year, they could have to repay up to the full benefit received.

Health and Prescription Insurance Tax

Ontario charges a tax on income for the health system. These amounts are collected through the income tax system, and do not determine eligiblity for public health care. The Ontario Health Premium is an additional amount charged on an individual's income tax that ranges from $300 for people with $20,000 of taxable income to $900 for high income earners. Individuals with less than $20,000 in taxable income are exempt.

Quebec also requires residents to obtain prescription insurance. When an individual does not have insurance, they must pay an income-derived premium. As these are income related, they are considered to be a tax on income under the law in Canada.

Other provinces, such as British Columbia and Alberta, charge premiums collected outside of the tax system for the provincial medicare systems. These are usually reduced or eliminated for low-income people.

Inheritance tax

Since the government of Brian Mulroney in the 1980s, Canada has had no inheritance taxes. Instead, inheritance is treated as a disposal subject to the same capital gains taxation as, for example, the sale of the asset.

International taxation

Canadian individuals and corporations pay income taxes based on their world-wide income. They are protected against double taxation through the foreign tax credit, which allows taxpayers to deduct from their Canadian income tax otherwise payable the income tax paid in other countries. A citizen who is currently not a resident of Canada may petition the CRA to change his status so that income from outside Canada is not taxed.

International Comparison (Personal Income Tax)

Comparison of taxes paid by a household earning the country's average wage

Country	Single no children	Married 2 children	Country	Single no children	Married 2 children
Australia	28.3%	16.0%	Korea	17.3%	16.2%
Austria	47.4%	35.5%	Luxembourg	35.3%	12.2%
Belgium	55.4%	40.3%	Mexico	18.2%	18.2%
Canada	31.6%	21.5%	Netherlands	38.6%	29.1%
Czech Republic	43.8%	27.1%	New Zealand	20.5%	14.5%
Denmark	41.4%	29.6%	Norway	37.3%	29.6%
Finland	44.6%	38.4%	Poland	43.6%	42.1%
France	50.1%	41.7%	Portugal	36.2%	26.6%
Germany	51.8%	35.7%	Slovak Republic	38.3%	23.2%
Greece	38.8%	39.2%	Spain	39.0%	33.4%
Hungary	50.5%	39.9%	Sweden	47.9%	42.4%
Iceland	29.0%	11.0%	Switzerland	29.5%	18.6%
Ireland	25.7%	8.1%	Turkey	42.7%	42.7%
Italy	45.4%	35.2%	United Kingdom	33.5%	27.1%
Japan	27.7%	24.9%	United States	29.1%	11.9%

Source: OECD, 2005 data [1]

Chapter 3

Taxpayer Bill of Rights

"You have to declare what you rob from the rich, but you can deduct what you give to the poor."

The Taxpayer Bill of Rights builds upon the Canada Revenue Agency's (CRA) corporate values of professionalism, respect, integrity and cooperation. It describes the treatment you are entitled to when dealing with the CRA. You can expect that the CRA will serve you with high standards of accuracy, professionalism, courteousness and fairness. The Taxpayer Bill of Rights also sets out the CRA Commitment to Small Business to ensure their interactions with the CRA are conducted as efficiently and effectively as possible.

1. You have the right to receive entitlements and to pay no more and no less than what is required by law.

You can expect to receive the benefits, credits and refunds to which you are entitled under the law and to pay no more and no less than the correct amount required under the law.

2. You have the right to service in both official languages.

You can expect us to communicate with you and provide services in the official language of your choice (English or French) on the

Internet, by telephone, in writing or at our designated bilingual offices.

3. You have the right to privacy and confidentiality.

You can expect us to protect the confidentiality of the information that you provide. Your information will be used only for purposes allowed by law. Only those persons who are authorized by law and who require the information to administer programs and legislation have the right to access your personal and financial information.

4. You have the right to a formal review and a subsequent appeal.

You are entitled to a formal review of your file if you believe that we have not applied the law correctly or that you have not received your full entitlements. Appeals officers who were not involved in the original decision will conduct a formal and impartial review. Filing an objection (an appeal in the case of assessments and rulings related to the Canada Pension Plan or Employment Insurance) will start the review by Agency appeals officers. If they do not resolve the matter to your satisfaction, you are entitled to appeal to the courts.

5. You have the right to be treated professionally, courteously, and fairly.

You can expect we will treat you courteously and with consideration at all times, including when we request information or arrange interviews and audits. Integrity, professionalism, respect and co-operation are our core values and reflect our commitment to giving you the best possible service. You can also expect us to listen to you, take your circumstances into account, and treat you fairly to make fair and impartial decisions in accordance with the law. We will explain our decision and inform you about your rights and obligations with respect to that decision.

6. You have the right to complete, accurate, clear, and timely information.

You can expect us to provide you with complete, accurate and timely information that will explain in plain language the laws and policies that apply to your situation, to help you get your entitlements and meet your obligations.

7. You have the right, as an individual, not to pay income tax amounts in dispute before you have had an impartial review.

You are entitled to withhold payment of assessed income tax amounts that you are disputing in a formal objection, other than source deductions, until you have had a formal review by the CRA or, if you have filed an appeal, until the Tax Court of Canada has issued its decision. If you appeal to a higher court, you will be able to provide equivalent security instead of paying the amount in dispute. However, in certain circumstances that are specified in the legislation, the CRA can exercise its authority to take collection action even though an objection or appeal has been filed.

8. You have the right to have the law applied consistently.

You can expect us to apply the law consistently so everyone gets their entitlements and pays the right amount. We will take your particular circumstances into account to the extent that the legislation we administer allows us to do so.

9. You have the right to lodge a service complaint and to be provided with an explanation of our findings.

You can expect that if you lodge a complaint about the service you receive from us, you will be listened to and given the opportunity to explain your situation. We will deal with your complaint promptly, impartially and in confidence, and we will provide you with an explanation of our findings.

10. You have the right to have the costs of compliance taken into account when administering tax legislation.

We recognize the need to keep to a minimum your costs, including your time and effort, that are incurred to comply with the tax and benefit legislation we administer while balancing our responsibility to administer the legislation efficiently and economically. We strive to make our dealings with you as straightforward and convenient as possible.

11. You have the right to expect us to be accountable.

You have the right to expect us to be accountable for what we do. When we make a decision about your tax or benefit affairs, we will explain that decision and inform you about your rights and obligations in respect of that decision. We are also accountable to Parliament, and through Parliament to Canadians, for what we do. We report to Parliament on our performance with respect to tax services and benefit programs and the results we achieve against our published service standards.

12. You have the right to relief from penalties and interest under tax legislation because of extraordinary circumstances.

You can expect us to consider your request to waive or cancel in whole or in part any penalty and interest charges if you were prevented from complying with your tax obligations because of circumstances beyond your control, e.g. a disaster such as a flood or fire, or if penalty or interest arose primarily because of erroneous actions of the CRA, e.g. material available to the public contained errors which led you to file incorrect returns or make incorrect payments based on incorrect information.

13. You have the right to expect us to publish our service standards and report annually.

You have the right to expect us to make our service standards publicly available for you to consult. Our service standards state the level of performance that you can reasonably expect to encounter in your dealings with us under normal circumstances. You can also expect us to measure our performance against our service standards and publish the results in the CRA Annual Report that is tabled in Parliament every year.

14. You have the right to expect us to warn you about questionable tax schemes in a timely manner.

You can expect the CRA to provide timely and relevant information about questionable tax schemes that the CRA intends to scrutinize so that you can recognize and avoid falling into tax schemes that could put you at odds with Canada's tax laws. We strive to provide information that will help you understand how to protect yourself against tax schemes and understand the consequences you may face as a result of your participation in tax schemes.

15. You have the right to be represented by a person of your choice.

You can get advice about your tax and benefit affairs from and be represented by a person of your choice. If you provide us with authorization, we will discuss your situation with the representative of your choice. However, it is important for you to be aware that you are legally responsible for your tax and benefit affairs even if you choose to obtain assistance or have someone act on your behalf.

The Canada Revenue Agency Commitment to Small Business

We endeavour to support the competitiveness of the Canadian business community by ensuring that your interactions with the Canada Revenue Agency (CRA) are conducted as efficiently and effectively as possible.

1. The CRA is committed to administering the tax system in a way that minimizes the costs of compliance for small businesses.

We recognize the need to keep to a minimum the time, effort and costs you incur to comply with tax and benefit legislation we administer, while balancing our responsibility to administer the legislation efficiently and economically. We strive to make our dealings with you as straightforward and convenient as possible.

2. The CRA is committed to working with all governments to streamline service, minimize cost, and reduce the compliance burden.

We work with other federal departments and provincial and territorial governments to determine areas where we can administer tax and benefit programs on their behalf or co-ordinate service delivery to reduce costs for both businesses and governments. We are committed to working with all governments to reduce the administrative and paper burden on small businesses to assist them to become more competitive.

3. The CRA is committed to providing service offerings that meet the needs of small businesses.

We strive to ensure that your interaction with the CRA is as quick, simple and effective as possible. We are continually improving our service offerings to businesses and the variety of channels through which these services are made available to businesses. Small businesses can now access CRA services on a 21/7 basis on the Internet or on a 24/7 basis through our comprehensive automated response systems.

4. The CRA is committed to conducting outreach activities that help small businesses comply with the legislation we administer.

We conduct community visits and other outreach programs to promote awareness of tax obligations and entitlements and help you comply with the requirements of the legislation we administer.

Some specific outreach programs are designed to provide assistance targeted to particular sectors or businesses. These educational and outreach activities enhance communication between the CRA and small businesses.

5. The CRA is committed to explaining how we conduct our business with small businesses.

We will clearly explain the steps we will follow when we conduct business with you. We will help you understand what to expect when we conduct an audit, undertake collection action, provide a ruling, review an objection in respect of a tax assessment, or conduct other program activities relating to the administration of tax and benefit legislation

Income Splitting Techniques to Reduce Income Tax

What is Income Splitting

Canada has a progressive income tax system - the more you earn the higher the rate of tax which you pay. Income splitting is a family tax planning technique designed to shift income from a high rate taxpayer to a lower rate taxpayer such as a spouse or children.

A number of different techniques can be used to accomplish this objective. However, you must be careful because Revenue Canada frowns on income splitting and there are provisions in the *Income Tax Act* designed to curtail it.

Tax Planning and Income Splitting Opportunities in Canada

As discussed in the attribution discussion, income splitting is only possible with certain types of income. Splitting arrangements may not always result in an even distribution of income throughout a family group. In addition, income splitting arrangements can be complex, expensive, and difficult to maintain. However, when there are family members in different tax brackets, income splitting can be a powerful tool.

Proper records must be kept when establishing an income splitting arrangement. In order to show that the lower income family member acquired investments, it is advisable to maintain separate bank accounts and keep detailed records. Avoid transfers between accounts through on-line banking and write cheques to establish a paper trail. Be sure to fully document the terms and repayment of any loans provided as well as documenting how any transfers of property occurred.

Tax Splitting / Saving Tips

Below is a list of common income splitting opportunities:

- The higher income earning spouse should pay all of the family expenses that are not deductible for tax purposes in order to make as much income for the lower income earning spouse available to invest. This includes paying the tax bill of the lower income spouse.
- Tuition fees do not have to be actually paid by the student to receive the tuition tax credit. A parent may pay the expense and the student may still claim the credit.
- If a related minor or spouse receives a gift or inheritance from a source that the income splitting rules would not have applied, the funds should be held in a separate account and "not" be used for household expenses.
- If a new business is started, allow lower income family members to acquire an equity position. Consult a professional for advice on structuring such an arrangement.
- If there is business income earned in the family to related corporation, the lower income spouse and children should be paid a reasonable salary for work performed in the business.
- If the CRAs prescribed rate of interest is lower than investment yields, it may be beneficial to lend funds at the prescribed rate to a family member who reinvests the funds.
- Property that has the potential to earn capital gains should be given to minor children rather than a spouse.
- Spousal RRSPs have a limited potential for income splitting. The goal should be to ensure both spouses have the same income in retirement.
- Maximize RRSPs by contributing to the lower income spouses RRSP.

- Lending funds to a spouse saves little money unless the amounts are in excess of $100,000.
- If funds are given to a child in their 17th year and a term deposit is acquired where the interest will pay in their 18th year. The interest will be tax in their hands in the following year
- If a child has employment income, lending funds up to an amount to which they would earn from employment, interest free, will free the child's employment income to earn investment income. The funds lent would then be used for their own purchases.
- Income earned from Canada child tax benefit payments invested in the child's name will not be attributed.
- Split your pension income with your spouse

This list is not exhaustive and it is recommended that you consult your accountant for advice.

Canadian Tax Issues During And After Three-Year Naturalization Period

Tax planning for new Permanent Residents of Canada is a critical part of the settlement process. If appropriate steps are taken while planning your move, the impact of Canadian taxation can be legally minimized or effectively eliminated. The two fundamental concepts basic to Canadian tax planning are as follows:

a) Canada taxes its residents on their worldwide income using Canadian Income tax rules and rates. If you are Canadaian Citizen and not residing in Canada then Canada does not tax you.

b) Canada taxes non-residents of Canada (including Canadian Citizens who are not resident in Canada) only on:

i) any employment income earned in Canada;

ii) any business income earned from carrying on a business in Canada;

iii) capital gains primarily attributable to Canadian real estate and shares in private Canadian companies; and

iv) certain types of Canadian source investment income such as interest, rents, dividends and royalties. This is done by the imposition of a withholding tax at a statutory rate of twenty-five percent, which may be reduced under applicable income tax agreements.

A Canadian citizen who departs Canada and becomes a "non-resident" for tax purposes will no longer be subject to Canadian taxation other than as described above. Neither the Canadian federal government nor any of its provincial governments impose any estate taxes or succession duties on death.

The income tax imposed on Canadian taxpayers is computed at a personal level. The Income Tax Act (Canada) provides for all the usual deductions and credits recognized in most industrial countries. Business losses and carry forwards are allowed in calculating "taxable income". Once taxable income has been determined, the "marginal tax rate" will apply. The tax rates are progressive with maximum rates varying from province to province. Capital gains are taxed at only seventy-five percent of full rates and dividends received from Canadian corporations by individuals receive favorable treatment. However, the maximum combined federal-provincial personal income tax rates generally range from fifty percent to fifty-eight percent depending on the province of residence at the end of the calendar year.

The Income Tax Act does allow an immigrant to shelter non-Canadian source income and capital gain for a period of up to sixty months after their arrival in Canada. The sixty-month period commences on January 1 of the calendar year during which the taxpayer becomes resident in Canada for tax purposes. Typically, income/capital gain-producing assets that are situated outside of Canada are transferred into an "offshore trust". A non-resident financial institution is used as trustee. All income and capital gains attributable to such assets that are earned by the trust, escape Canadian tax during the period that the individual is a Permanent Resident of Canada and is in the qualification period of Canadian Citizenship. This "tax holiday" expires at the end of the sixty-month period. If the trust continues in place thereafter and the person remains resident in Canada for tax purposes, the trust itself will become a resident taxpayer and liable for Canadian taxation on its worldwide income.

If, however, the Permanent Resident obtains Canadian Citizenship within the five-year tax holiday window and then departs Canada after obtaining Canadian Citizenship, the income and capital gain produced by the offshore trust will never be taxed by the Canadian government. Those who choose to remain resident in Canada as Canadian residents and citizens beyond the five year period, may choose to reacquire the assets from the offshore trust at that point for a "stepped up" tax basis. They will then have a new basis equal to the fair market value of the assets at the end of the five-year period. In addition, they may wish to explore one of several other strategies to extend the "tax holiday" period.

In conclusion, Canada is a very attractive destination. One must be aware that it is a potentially high tax country where improper or absent tax advice can result in high worldwide tax liability. As Canadian Immigration officials are neither qualified nor obligated to provide you with any advice relating to the structuring of your financial or tax affairs, it is recommend that you receive proper written legal advice. If properly done, establishing residence and domicile in Canada may be a more appropriate solution for someone who for business or family reasons cannot live in an island tax haven.

Canada is not just for clean air, mountains and efficiency. Canada can also be called the Switzerland of the North.

CN Tower Toronto

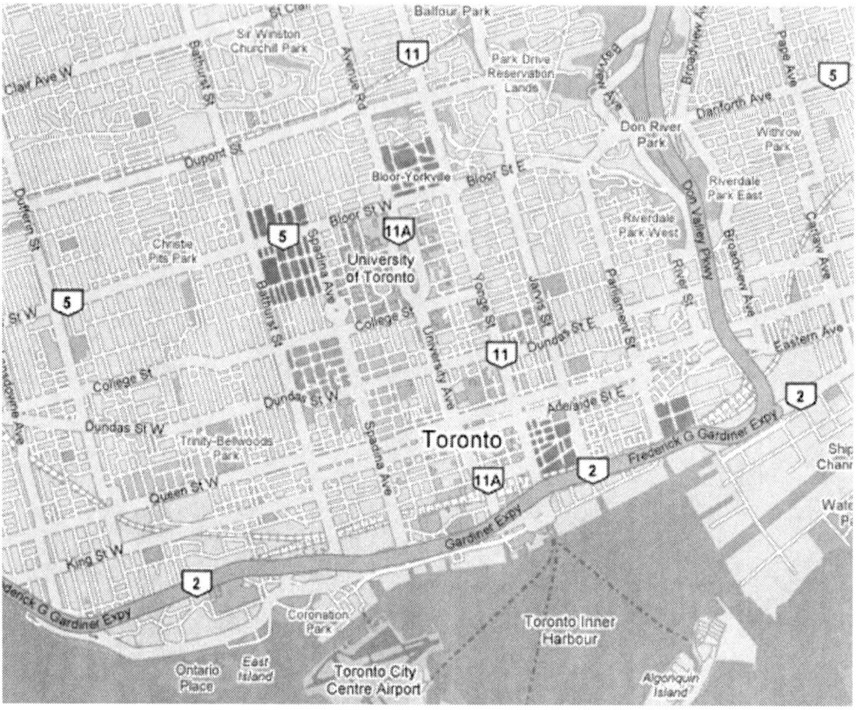

Paul Martin (21st Prime Minister of Canada) with Prime Minister of India (Dr. Manmohan Singh)

SUGGESTED ARTICLES TO READ FOR TAX SAVINGS / FINANCIAL PALNNING

DAVID S. LESPERANCE BARRISTER & SOLICITOR

The following articles by David S. Lesperance

http://www.globalrelocate.com/articles.htm

CANADA

1. A non-traditional Tax Haven

U.S. - UNITED STATES

1. H. Alger

2. Can expats be banned from the US?

3. Leaving on a Jet Plane

4. Myths and Reality

5. Your Passport Portfolio

6. Strategies

Chapter 4

Taxpayers' Ombudsman

What is the Taxpayers' Ombudsman?

The Taxpayers' Ombudsman is an independent and impartial officer who is appointed to look into complaints about the service provided by the Canada Revenue Agency (CRA).

The Taxpayers' Ombudsman operates at arm's length from the CRA and reports directly to the Minister of National Revenue. The Taxpayers' Ombudsman submits an annual report to the Minister, which is tabled in Parliament, and may issue other reports and/or recommendations concerning any issue within the Taxpayers' Ombudsman mandate.

The Taxpayers' Ombudsman is the final level of review and complements existing service-related complaint resolution mechanisms internal to the CRA.

Mandate of the Taxpayers' Ombudsman

The Taxpayers' Ombudsman's role is to:

- conduct impartial and independent reviews of service-related complaints about the CRA;
- ensure that the CRA respects the service rights outlined in the Taxpayer Bill of Rights;
- facilitate taxpayers' access to assistance within the CRA;
- identify and review systemic and emerging service-related issues within the CRA that have a negative impact on taxpayers; and
- provide advice and make recommendations to the Minister of National Revenue about service-related matters in the CRA.

Complaints we can review

The Taxpayers' Ombudsman will review complaints that are related to **service** provided by the CRA.

A service-related complaint includes:

- mistakes, which could refer to misunderstandings, omissions, or oversights;
- undue delays;
- poor or misleading information; and

- staff behaviour.

The Taxpayers' Ombudsman will also review complaints where any of the following service rights outlined in the Taxpayer Bill of Rights may not have been respected by the CRA:

- The right to be treated professionally, courteously, and fairly.
- The right to complete, accurate, clear, and timely information from the CRA.
- The right to lodge a service complaint and to be provided with an explanation of the CRA findings.
- The right to have the costs of compliance taken into account when tax legislation is administered.
- The right to expect the CRA to be accountable.
- The right to expect the CRA to publish service standards and report annually.
- The right to expect the CRA to warn you about questionable tax schemes in a timely manner.
- The right to be represented by a person of your choice.

The Taxpayers' Ombudsman will not become involved in matters related to legislation or interpretation of tax policy. Since there are already well-defined mechanisms for dealing with these kinds of issues, we will provide advice on what you should do if your complaint is outside the Taxpayers' Ombudsman's mandate.

Before contacting us...

Before contacting the Taxpayers' Ombudsman, we suggest you follow these steps:

1. Try to resolve the issue with the CRA employee you have been dealing with.
2. If you are not satisfied, talk to the employee's supervisor.
3. If you are still not satisfied with the way your issue is being handled, file a formal complaint with the CRA. Information about the CRA service-related complaint process can be found in pamphlet RC4420, *Information on CRA - Service Complaints*. You can get any forms or publications you need from the CRA Web site at cra.gc.ca/forms or by calling 1-800-959-2221.

Making a complaint to the Ombudsman

If you are not satisfied with the way your service-related complaint was handled by the CRA, submit the details of your complaint to the Taxpayers' Ombudsman using our complaint form. There is a copy of this form in the middle of this guide. You can also access a fillable version of this form by visiting our Web site at taxpayersrights.gc.ca.

Send the completed form along with any supporting documentation by **fax to 1-866-586-3855**, or by mail to:

Taxpayers' Ombudsman
Suite 724
50 O'Connor Street
Ottawa ON K1P 6L2

Alternate formats are also available by calling the Taxpayers' Ombudsman at **1-866-586-3839** weekdays (except holidays) from 8:15 a.m. to 4:30 p.m. (Eastern Time).

Note: *There are no costs associated with filing a complaint or for any service provided by the Taxpayers' Ombudsman.*

General tips when submitting a complaint

- Keep a record of events and a copy of any letters you sent to and received from the CRA. If you spoke to someone on the telephone, we suggest that you make a note of what was said and the name of the person you spoke to.
- Be clear about what you would like to happen as a result of making the complaint. Are you looking for an apology, or a service that should have been provided but was not?
- Complete all the applicable areas of the complaint form.
- Sign and date Section 3 of the form, "Consent to disclose information," to authorize the exchange of information between the Taxpayers' Ombudsman and the CRA for the purpose of reviewing your complaint.
- If you are designating a representative to act on your behalf, provide the identifying information for your representative. Both you and your representative must sign and date Section 4 of the form, "Third party authorization."

If you need help filling out the complaint form, you can call our office at 1-866-586-3839 and one of our staff members will be pleased to assist you.

What to expect when we receive your complaint

1. Acknowledgement

We will acknowledge the receipt of your complaint. We will also provide you with a reference number to use if you need to contact us regarding the case.

2. Screening

If we cannot review your complaint, we will let you know why and we will refer you, as needed, to the appropriate area within the CRA, or suggest who might be able to help you.

3. Review process

An examination officer will be assigned to your case. We will conduct an impartial review of your complaint based on all the available information in order to decide what we believe is fair and reasonable in the circumstances of the case.

The examination officer will keep you informed throughout the process. You can also contact us and speak to the examination officer assigned to your file.

4. Conclusion

At the end of our review, we will send you and the CRA the outcome of our review along with our recommendation, if applicable. We will follow up with the CRA on any recommendations that we make.

As part of our recommendations to the CRA, we can suggest that the CRA:

- give further reasons for a decision;
- correct a misunderstanding, omission, or oversight;
- offer an apology;
- change a policy or procedure;
- make changes to systems or applications;
- review its service standards; or
- consider further staff training.

Privacy and sharing of information with the CRA

In order to fully review your complaint, the Taxpayers' Ombudsman may need to share information with the CRA. We will only share information with your consent. The information collected is treated with confidentiality.

Beautiful Al-Islam Mosque, Maple, Ontario, Canada

Symbols of Canada
Les Symboles du Canada
FLAG • DRAPEAU
COAT OF ARMS • ARMOIRIES
FLOWER • FLEUR
BIRD • OISEAU
ALBERTA
BRITISH COLUMBIA
COLOMBIE-BRITANNIQUE
MANITOBA
NEW BRUNSWICK
NOUVEAU-BRUNSWICK
NEWFOUNDLAND AND LABRADOR
TERRE-NEUVE-ET-LABRADOR
NORTHWEST TERRITORIES
TERRITOIRES DU NORD-OUEST

Chapter 5

What Are The Income Tax Rates In Canada For 2008?

These are the rates that an individual will use when completing their 2008 income tax and benefit return. The information may change during the year to reflect updates to the law.

Federal tax rates for 2008 are:

- 15% **on the first** $37,885 of taxable income, +
- 22% **on the next** $37,884 of taxable income (on the portion of taxable income between $37,885 and $75,769), +
- 26% **on the next** $47,415 of taxable income (on the portion of taxable income between $75,769 and $123,184), +
- 29% of taxable income **over** $123,184.

•

The chart below reproduces the first calculation that has to be made on *Page 2 of Schedule 1* of the tax package to calculate net federal tax. Page 1 is used to calculate federal non-refundable tax credits.

Federal Tax On Taxable Income Manual Calculation Chart

	Use this column if your taxable income is **$37,885 or less**	Use this column if your taxable income is **more than** $37,885, **but not more than** $75,769	Use this column if your taxable income is **more than** $75,769, **but not more than** $123,184	Use this column if your taxable income is **more than $123,184**	
Enter your taxable income from line 260 of your return					**1**
Base amount	– 0	– 37,885	– 75,769	– 123,184	**2**
Line 1 minus line 2 (this amount cannot be negative)	=	=	=	=	**3**
Federal tax rate	× 15%	× 22%	× 26%	× 29%	**4**
Multiply the amount on line 3 by the tax rate on line 4	=	=	=	=	**5**
Tax on the amount from line 2	+ 0	+ 5,683	+ 14,017	+ 26,345	**6**
Add lines 5 and 6	=	=	=	=	**7**

Provincial/Territorial Tax Rates For 2008

Under the current tax on income method, tax for all provinces (except Quebec) and territories is calculated the same way as federal tax.

Form 428 is used to calculate this provincial or territorial tax. Provincial or territorial specific non-refundable tax credits are also calculated on Form 428.

For complete details, see the *Provincial or Territorial information and forms* in your 2008 tax package.

Provincial / Territorial tax rates (combined chart)

Provinces / Territories	Rate(s)
Newfoundland and Labrador	8.7% on the first $30,215 of taxable income, + 13.8% on the next $30,214, + 16.5% on the amount over $60,429
Prince Edward Island	9.8% on the first $31,984 of taxable income, + 13.8% on the next $31,985, + 16.7% on the amount over $63,969
Nova Scotia	8.79% on the first $29,590 of taxable income, + 14.95% on the next $29,590, + 16.67% on the next $33,820 + 17.5% on the amount over $93,000
New Brunswick	10.12% on the first $34,836 of taxable income, + 15.48% on the next $34,837, + 16.8% on the next $43,600, + 17.95% on the amount over $113,273
Ontario	6.05% on the first $36,020 of taxable income, + 9.15% on the next $36,021, + 11.16% on the amount over $72,041

Manitoba	10.9% on the first $30,544 of taxable income, + 12.75% on the next $35,456, + 17.4% on the amount over $66,000
Saskatchewan	11% on the first $39,135 of taxable income, + 13% on the next $72,679, + 15% on the amount over $111,814
Alberta	10% of taxable income

British Columbia	5.24% on the first $35,016 of taxable income, + 7.98% on the next $35,017, + 10.5% on the next $10,373, + 12.29% on the next $17,230, + 14.7% on the amount over $97,636
Yukon	7.04% on the first $37,885 of taxable income, + 9.68% on the next $37,884, + 11.44% on the next $47,415, + 12.76% on the amount over $123,184
Northwest Territories	5.9% on the first $35,986 of taxable income, + 8.6% on the next $35,987, + 12.2% on the next $45,038, + 14.05% on the amount over $117,011
Nunavut	4% on the first $37,885 of taxable income, + 7% on the next $37,884, + 9% on the next $47,415, + 11.5% on the amount over $123,184

Canadian House Prices

Average House Prices In Canada

One of the major attractions of a move to Canada is the cost of housing compared with other western countries

As happens everywhere, prices are higher in Canada's big cities than they are in the surrounding towns.

Canada's highest house prices are found on the west coast in Vancouver / British Columbia, where the country's mildest weather is found.

Severe winter weather or remoteness from major markets usually results in low house prices - for example property prices are low in Manitoba and Prince Edward Island.

In 2007 prices in booming Alberta rose above prices in Ontario for the first time and, in the same vein, prices in Calgary rose above those in Toronto.

Canadian Cities Average House Prices November 2007

Province	Average House Price
Vancouver, BC	$566,000
Calgary, Alb	$400,000
Toronto, Ont	$395,000
Ottawa, Ont	$277,000
Montreal, Que	$242,000
Halifax, NS	$209,000
Regina, Sask	$200,000
Fredericton, NB	$131,000

Canadian Provinces -Average House Prices- November 2007

Province	Average House Price
British Columbia	$453,000
Alberta	$353,000
Ontario	$313,000
Quebec	$217,000
Saskatchewan	$194,000
Nova Scotia	$175,000
Manitoba	$173,000
Newfoundland / Labrador	$146,000
Prince Edward Island	$137,000
New Brunswick	$134,000
Canadian Average	$314,000

How is Canada Faring Compared to Other Industrialized Countries?

Overall, fairly well. No other G-7 country has run seven consecutive surpluses. Canada is the only G-7 member to run a surplus in 2004.

The United States has gone from substantial surpluses four years ago to a record deficit of $455 billion this year.

Among G-7 countries, Canada's debt burden moved from second-highest in the mid-1990s to second-lowest in 2003. The Organization for Economic Co-operation and Development predicts Canada's debt burden will soon be the lowest among G-7 nations.

REPORT CARD

Economy

Rank	Country	Grade
1	Ireland	A
2	Switzerland	A
3	Norway	A
4	Sweden	A
5	Netherlands	A
6	Finland	B
7	U.S.	B
8	U.K.	B
9	Belgium	B
10	Denmark	B
11	Canada	B
12	Australia	B
13	Austria	C
14	Japan	C
15	France	D
16	Italy	D
17	Germany	D

Note: Data for the most recent year available used.
Source: The Conference Board of Canada.

REPORT CARD

Environment

Rank	Country	Grade
1	Sweden	A
2	Finland	A
3	Norway	A
4	Switzerland	A
5	U.K.	B
6	France	B
7	Italy	B
8	Austria	C
9	Germany	C
10	Ireland	C
11	Denmark	C
12	Belgium	C
13	Netherlands	C
14	Japan	C
15	Canada	C
16	Australia	D
17	U.S.	D

Note: Data for the most recent year available used.
Source: The Conference Board of Canada.

REPORT CARD

Innovation

Rank	Country	Grade
1	U.S.	A
2	Switzerland	A
3	Ireland	A
4	Japan	B
5	Germany	B
6	Sweden	B
7	Netherlands	B
8	U.K.	B
9	France	C
10	Finland	C
11	Denmark	C
12	Belgium	C
13	Canada	D
14	Australia	D
15	Austria	D
16	Italy	D
17	Norway	D

Note: Data for the most recent year available used.
Source: The Conference Board of Canada.

REPORT CARD

Society

Rank	Country	Grade
1	Denmark	A
2	Norway	A
3	Netherlands	A
4	Sweden	A
5	Switzerland	B
6	Austria	B
7	Germany	B
8	Finland	B
9	France	B
10	Canada	B
11	Belgium	C
12	Ireland	C
13	Australia	C
14	Italy	C
15	U.K.	D
16	Japan	D
17	U.S.	D

Note: Data for the most recent year available used.
Source: The Conference Board of Canada.

REPORT CARD

Education and Skills

Rank	Country	Grade
1	Finland	A
2	Canada	B
3	Japan	B
4	Switzerland	B
5	Sweden	B
6	Australia	B
7	Germany	B
8	Netherlands	B
9	Belgium	B
10	Denmark	C
11	U.K.	C
12	Austria	C
13	Ireland	C
14	France	C
15	Norway	C
16	U.S.	C
17	Italy	D

Note: Data for the most recent year available used.
Source: The Conference Board of Canada.

REPORT CARD

Health

Rank	Country	Grade
1	Japan	A
2	Switzerland	A
3	Italy	A
4	France	A
5	Sweden	A
6	Norway	B
7	Australia	B
8	Germany	B
9	Canada	B
10	Austria	C
11	Finland	C
12	Netherlands	C
13	Ireland	D
14	U.K.	D
15	U.S.	D
16	Denmark	D

Note: Data are not available for Belgium. For the rest, data for the most recent year available were used.
Source: The Conference Board of Canada.

Ottawa Tops List of Best Cdn Cities To Live in, Toronto Plunges in Rankings

High housing prices and crime are among the reasons for Toronto's plunge from #12 to #51 in an annual survey of the country's most liveable cities.

Ottawa topped *MoneySense* magazine's third annual list of Canada's Best Places To Live, which studied 154 communities and ranked them on a range of factors, among them economic, environmental, and social.

Six cities made the top ten list for the second year in a row - Ottawa, Ont., Victoria, B.C., Fredericton, N.B., Kingston, Ont., Moncton, N.B. and Halifax, N.S. - while four - Levis, Que., Winnipeg, Man., Burlington, Ont., and Vancouver, B.C. are new additions.

MoneySense also ranked the cities on what they had to offer in terms of weather, places to retire, and affordability.

"We look beyond pretty scenery or hot restaurants to find the places that deliver the best quality of life to residents," says *MoneySense* editor Ian McGugan. "Our methodology spans everything from home prices and weather to crime rates and the availability of medical care."

Toronto was one of the biggest sliders on the list, due to its flat population growth, relatively high crime rate and soaring housing prices in relation to income. On the flip side, Swift Current, Sask. jumped from #61 to #22, and Estevan, Sask. climbed from #68 to #34, their rise due to strong local economies and lower crime rates.

As far as how other GTA-area communities ranked, Burlington was tops overall at #8, Mississauga and Guelph came in at #11 and #12. Oakville made it to #26.

Overall winner Ottawa didn't actually make the top 10 in any of the individual categories, but fared quite well in all the categories, which is what put it atop the heap.

Top 10

1. **Ottawa-Gatineau**
2. **Victoria B.C.**
3. **Fredericton, N.B.**
4. **Kingston, Ont.**
5. **Levis, Que.**
6. **Moncton, N.B.**
7. **Winnipeg, Man.**
8. **Burlington, Ont.**
9. **Halifax, N.S.**
10. **Vancouver B.C.**

For a detailed description of the study and how other cities finished, see the complete rankings at www.moneysense.ca.

Chapter 6

Gays And Lesbians

Gays And Lesbians Can Get Married in Canada

Gays and Lesbians can get married in Canada from other parts of the world. There is no residency requirement to get married in Canada. This article is meant to provide you with basic information about getting married in Canada. Be sure to check in with local officials when you choose your wedding destination.

Also, different provinces have different rules and regulations regarding marriage. Check out the resources at the end of the article for more specific information.

Here's How:

1. Apply for a license. In the following provinces **both** of you need to apply for the marriage license: Alberta, Manitoba, New Brunswick, Northwest Territory, Nunavut, Ontario, Prince Edward Island, Quebec, Saskatchewan and Yukon. In the following provinces **either** party can apply for the marriage license: British Columbia, Nova Scotia, Newfoundland and Labrador.
2. **Locate your documents**

   Each locality has different paperwork requirements, but in general you will need: proof of age, photo id, and birth certificates. If one of you has been previously married you must show proof of death or divorce. You must have the original divorce decree when you apply for the marriage licence. A copy is not accepted.

3. **Wait**

Quebec has a 20 day waiting period between the time you apply for a license and when you can get married. Alberta, British Columbia, New Brunswick, Northwest Territory, Nunavut, Ontario and Prince Edward Island have no waiting period. Others vary from 24 hours to five days. Check with the local municipality.

4. **Pay**

Marriage license fees vary from place to place. You also may need to pay the officiant and for a marriage certificate.

5. **Decide who will perform the ceremony**

You can get married in Canada with either a civil or religious ceremony. Again, different regions have different rules about who can perform civil ceremonies. Most communities have marriage commissioners, judges or justices of the peace to perform your wedding.

Religious clergy who are registered to perform marriages in Canada can marry you in a religious ceremony.

6. **Step to the Aisle and say "I do!"**
7. **What if you want to divorce?**

Although Canada has no residency requirement for marriage, it does have one for divorce. At least one partner must reside in Canada for one year to be eligible for divorce. American courts, who do not recognize the marriage, are not likely to grant you a divorce.

8. **Check out local regulations**

   Alberta
   http://www.servicealberta.gov.ab.ca
9. British Columbia
   http://www.vs.gov.bc.ca/marriage/index.html
10. Manitoba
    http://vitalstats.gov.mb.ca//GettingMarried.html
11. New Brunswick
    http://www.gnb.ca
12. New Foundland & Labrador
    http://www.gs.gov.nl.ca/gs/vs/marriage.stm
13. Nova Scotia
    http://www.gov.ns.ca/snsmr/vstat/certificates/getting_married.asp
14. Nunavut
    http://www.gov.nu.ca
15. Ontario
    http://www.cbs.gov.on.ca
16. PEI
    http://www.gov.pe.ca
17. Quebec
    http://www.justice.gouv.qc.ca/english/publications/generale/maria-a.htm
18. Saskatchewan
    http://www.health.gov.sk.ca/vital-statistics
19. Yukon
    http://www.hss.gov.yk.ca/programs/vitalstats/marriage/

Annual Pride Parade Toronto

WE MARCH FOR
PEACE

Kennedy

Hudson's Bay Company

VIP
BAR & GRILL
BILLIARDS 22 POOL TABLES
O'Keefe Lane
Just Married

Tips:

1. You cannot marry a same-sex partner in Canada if you are already married.
2. You cannot get married in Canada if you have a civil union in Vermont or Connecticut.
3. Even if you marry in Canada, the United States government is not required to recognize your marriage. The Federal Defense of Marriage Act defines marriage as solely between a man and a woman. Many states have passed similar legislation.
4. Getting married in Canada will not allow you to sponsor your spouse for U.S. citizenship.
5. After getting married, consult legal advice before filing your taxes.

What You Need:

- A willing partner
- Birth Certificate or Passport
- Photo ID
- Proof of Divorce or spouse's death if applicable
- Social Security Numbers
- Written parental consent if under 18
- Canadian money for any fees
- Two Witnesses

Ellen DeGeneres and "Arrested Development" star Portia de Rossi are getting married! According to an audience member at the Thursday night taping of the Ellen show, Ellen DeGeneres herself made the announcement that she and girlfriend Portia de Rossi are planning a wedding.

Time for a Paradigm Shift

Tax and spend! Tax and spend! That has been the mantra for governments since time immemorial. Even the Bible mentions taxes - render unto Caesar! Caesar taxes. Caesar spends. No wonder then that today we continue to look on government as an agency that taxes and spends. Most people even think this is normal and can't conceive of any other way of financing government.

True, some have revolted against taxes. Lady Godiva. The noblemen who fought for the Magna Carta. The Boston Tea Party. But these revolts have been against oppressive taxation, unfair taxation, or taxation without representation. None were revolts against the idea of taxes themselves. Heck, we need government. Government needs to be financed. Ergo, we need taxes.

Although the anarchists among us might dispute whether we even need government, let's take as a given that we do, in fact, need it. And let's take as a given that government needs to be financed. Does it follow that we need taxes? The old paradigm says yes! But what if we looked at it a different way? What if we approached the financing of government the way an individual looks at financing his retirement?

Ah! Now there's a paradigm shift! An individual does not continue working throughout his whole life. He plans for a time when he will leave the workforce to enjoy his senior years in leisure. He still needs to eat. He still needs shelter. He still needs to get around. He still needs to spend. That does not change although seniors often have lower expenditures.

All during his working life, the individual's mantra was earn and spend, earn and spend just as the government's is tax and spend, tax and spend. But the individual knows he must plan for retirement, so along with earn and spend, he takes a portion of his earnings to save and invest. After 40-50 years of working, if he has been wise and frugal and followed a well thought out savings and investment plan, he will have built up a nest egg that will generate an income to live on. And if he has been very wise, he will be able to live out his senior years in great comfort, enjoying trips, dinners out, evenings at the theatre and so on.

Right now Canada is blessed in that our government is running a substantial surplus. What if government followed the same plan as an individual? What if government saved that money and invested it? What if the government built up a nest egg over time large enough to generate enough income to cover the cost of the government itself?

By my calculations, the government could achieve that goal in under fifty years. In just two generations the government of Canada could abolish the personal income tax *forever!* From there it could move to eventually eliminate all taxes.

Here are the facts:

Canada has run a surplus since 1998 after years of profligate spending. These surpluses have varied year to year but for fiscal 2006, Canada ran its largest surplus ever, over $13 billion. The government is directing the entire sum to retiring the accumulated debt, which is not a bad thing. But here is a better idea.

Why not take some of the surplus and put it into savings and invest it? Why not build up a nest egg large enough that the entire cost of government can be funded out of investment income?

Government funding out of investment income? Not as outlandish an idea as it may seem. Since 1989 (the earliest year for which Statistics Canada has downloadable government fiscal information), investment income has been prominent in the government's accounts. The lowest figure is $4,536 million in 1997. The highest has been $7,485 million in 2003. The average has been $6,001 million and change.

The $5,523 million of investment income in 1989 accounted for 4.94% of all government revenues. The $6,613 million of investment income for 2006 accounted for just 2.88% of all government revenues as the total revenues more than doubled in those 18 years while the investment income remained relatively unchanged.

If the government commits to re-investing just the approximately $6 billion of investment income into further investments, compounding growth over time, the government will eventually be able to be self-financing. This is especially so since the government doesn't eventually cease to exist so its time horizon for saving and investing is unlimited whereas individuals have a time horizon of 45 to 50 years.

The table below shows the government's revenues, revenue from all income taxes, revenue from personal income taxes, revenue from investment income, expenditures and surpluses since 1998. Click to link to see the data for all the years from **1989 to 2006**.

Year	1998	1999	2000	2001	2002	2003	2004	2005	2006
Revenues	168,214	172,595	184,018	197,303	195,881	195,091	203,549	216,443	229,660
Income Taxes	101,265	103,150	112,933	122,318	120,560	114,859	123,821	133,248	144,562
Personal Income Tax	76,139	78,258	85,437	89,183	91,435	88,372	92,704	98,340	105,742
Investment Income	4,710	5,549	6,328	7,060	6,952	7,485	6,839	6,572	6,613
Expenditures	163,706	169,808	177,019	188,090	188,533	193,427	201,433	211,324	216,156
Deficit/Surplus	4,507	2,786	6,999	9,213	7,348	1,665	2,115	5,120	13,504

The growth in government expenditures from 1989 to 2006 averaged 2.72% a year. From 1989 to 2006 it grew at an average of 3.55% a year. The longer time period included years where the government actually managed to cut expenditures - 1994, 1997 and 1998.

Let's assume that the average increase in government expenditure since 1998 represents a correct assessment of the likely future growth of government expenditures from both inflation and organic growth due to population growth and net immigration.

Let's consider several goals starting with the elimination of the personal income tax. The personal income tax as a percentage of government revenue in 2006 was 46.04%. Let's assume that personal income taxes will continue to contribute the same percentage to revenues until our nest egg is able to take over fully as a replacement for this revenue.

The table below shows how long it would take to build up a nest egg sufficient to do that for various parameters. Explanation of the columns is as follows:

- Column 1: Number of years that have passed since base year 2006
- Column 2: The Year

- Column 3: Projected personal income taxes collected by the federal using 2006 as a base year and considering it will grow at 3.55% a year to accommodate growing population and inflation

- Column 4: Value of nest egg growing at 10% a year with $6 billion new funds added each year

- Column 5: Value of nest egg growing at 12% a year with $6 billion new funds added each year

- Column 6: Value of nest egg growing at 15% a year with $6 billion new funds added each year

- Column 7: Value of nest egg growing at 20% a year with $6 billion new funds added each year

- Column 8: Size of nest egg needed to fund personal income taxes if it generates 6% a year

- Column 9: Size of nest egg needed to fund personal income taxes if it generates 8% a year

- Column 10: Size of nest egg needed to fund personal income taxes if it generates 10% a year

# of Years	Year	Personal Income Tax	10% Growth	12% Growth	15% Growth	20% Growth	Nest egg needed at 6%	Nest egg needed at 8%	Nest egg needed at 10%
	2006	$105,742	$6,000	$6,000	$6,000	$6,000	$1,762,367	$1,321,775	$1,057,420
1	2007	$109,496	$12,600	$12,720	$12,900	$13,200	$1,824,931	$1,368,698	$1,094,958
2	2008	$113,383	$19,860	$20,246	$20,835	$21,840	$1,889,716	$1,417,287	$1,133,829
3	2009	$117,408	$27,846	$28,676	$29,960	$32,208	$1,956,801	$1,467,600	$1,174,080
22	2028	$227,798	$477,258	$627,617	$955,658	$1,957,421	$3,796,632	$2,847,474	$2,277,979
23	2029	$235,885	$530,984	$708,931	$1,105,007	$2,354,905	$3,931,413	$2,948,560	$2,358,848
24	2030	$244,259	$590,082	$800,003	$1,276,758	$2,831,886	$4,070,978	$3,053,233	$2,442,587
25	2031	$252,930	$655,091	$902,004	$1,474,272	$3,404,264	$4,215,498	$3,161,623	$2,529,299
26	2032	$261,909	$726,600	$1,016,244	$1,701,413	$4,091,117	$4,365,148	$3,273,861	$2,619,089
27	2033	$271,207	$805,260	$1,144,193	$1,962,624	$4,915,340	$4,520,111	$3,390,083	$2,712,066
28	2034	$280,834	$891,786	$1,287,497	$2,263,018	$5,904,408	$4,680,574	$3,510,431	$2,808,345
29	2035	$290,804	$986,964	$1,447,996	$2,608,471	$7,091,289	$4,846,735	$3,635,051	$2,908,041
30	2036	$301,128	$1,091,661	$1,627,756	$3,005,742	$8,515,547	$5,018,794	$3,764,095	$3,011,276
31	2037	$311,818	$1,206,827	$1,829,086	$3,462,603	$10,224,657	$5,196,961	$3,897,721	$3,118,177
32	2038	$322,887	$1,333,509	$2,054,577	$3,987,993	$12,275,588	$5,381,453	$4,036,090	$3,228,872
33	2039	$334,350	$1,472,860	$2,307,126	$4,592,192	$14,736,706	$5,572,495	$4,179,371	$3,343,497
34	2040	$346,219	$1,626,146	$2,589,981	$5,287,021	$17,690,047	$5,770,318	$4,327,739	$3,462,191
35	2041	$358,510	$1,794,761	$2,906,779	$6,086,074	$21,234,056	$5,975,165	$4,481,374	$3,585,099
36	2042	$371,237	$1,980,237	$3,261,592	$7,004,985	$25,486,867	$6,187,283	$4,640,462	$3,712,370
37	2043	$384,416	$2,184,261	$3,658,983	$8,061,733	$30,590,241	$6,406,932	$4,805,199	$3,844,159
38	2044	$398,063	$2,408,687	$4,104,061	$9,276,993	$36,714,289	$6,634,378	$4,975,783	$3,980,627
39	2045	$412,194	$2,655,555	$4,602,549	$10,674,542	$44,063,147	$6,869,898	$5,152,424	$4,121,939
40	2046	$426,827	$2,927,111	$5,160,854	$12,281,723	$52,881,776	$7,113,779	$5,335,335	$4,268,268
41	2047	$441,979	$3,225,822	$5,786,157	$14,129,982	$63,464,132	$7,366,319	$5,524,739	$4,419,791
42	2048	$457,669	$3,554,404	$6,486,496	$16,255,479	$76,162,958	$7,627,823	$5,720,867	$4,576,694
43	2049	$473,917	$3,915,845	$7,270,875	$18,699,801	$91,401,550	$7,898,611	$5,923,958	$4,739,166
44	2050	$490,741	$4,313,429	$8,149,380	$21,510,771	$109,687,860	$8,179,011	$6,134,259	$4,907,407
45	2051	$508,162	$4,750,772	$9,133,306	$24,743,386	$131,631,432	$8,469,366	$6,352,025	$5,081,620
46	2052	$526,202	$5,231,849	$10,235,303	$28,460,894	$157,963,718	$8,770,029	$6,577,522	$5,262,017
47	2053	$544,882	$5,761,034	$11,469,539	$32,736,028	$189,562,461	$9,081,365	$6,811,024	$5,448,819
48	2054	$564,225	$6,343,137	$12,851,883	$37,652,433	$227,480,954	$9,403,753	$7,052,815	$5,642,252
49	2055	$584,255	$6,983,451	$14,400,109	$43,306,298	$272,983,145	$9,737,586	$7,303,190	$5,842,552
50	2056	$604,996	$7,687,796	$16,134,123	$49,808,242	$327,585,773	$10,083,271	$7,562,453	$6,049,962
51	2057	$626,474	$8,462,576	$18,076,217	$57,285,479	$393,108,928	$10,441,227	$7,830,920	$6,264,736
52	2058	$648,713	$9,314,834	$20,251,363	$65,884,300	$471,736,714	$10,811,890	$8,108,918	$6,487,134
53	2059	$671,743	$10,252,317	$22,687,527	$75,772,946	$566,090,056	$11,195,713	$8,396,784	$6,717,428
54	2060	$695,590	$11,283,549	$25,416,030	$87,144,887	$679,314,068	$11,593,160	$8,694,870	$6,955,896
55	2061	$720,283	$12,417,903	$28,471,954	$100,222,620	$815,182,881	$12,004,718	$9,003,538	$7,202,831

This table has been truncated. Click for a complete 75 year version.

As our parameters, we are considering four different rates of return on our investment while the nest egg is growing and three different lower rates of return once the target nest egg has been achieved (assuming the government, like retiring seniors, moves into more conservative investments at this point.)

The rates of return for the growing nest egg are 10%, 12%, 15% and 20%. The rates of return after switching to a more conservative style is varied between 6%, 8% and 10%.

In the table above, the yellow bars represent the 10% return after switching to a conservative style option. The green bars represent the 8% return and the blue bar represents the 6% return.

With a 20% growth portfolio, the required nest egg to eliminate personal income tax based on a 10% return after target is reached is

24 years. With the 15% portfolio, the target is reached at 31 years. With the 12% growth portfolio it's reached after 38 years and with the 10% growth portfolio, the target is reached after 47 years.

Assuming the worst scenario...the 10% growth portfolio to achieve the target and a reversion to a conservative 6% growth after the target is reached, it would take 55 years to reach the point where the government of Canada could effectively eliminate personal income tax.

A possible and perhaps probable outcome is somewhere between the best and worst scenarios here, namely a return of 12% while growing and a reversion to 8% growth once the target is achieved. That would take 41 years.

Eliminating personal income tax within two generations is achievable.

Swami Narayan Temple , Canada

What would this nest egg be invested in?

Lest these rates be considered unrealistic, consider the following:

Of Canada's 6769 mutual funds, only two had a 15 year track record average of 20% or better. There was only one that did better than 20% average over a ten year period. But there were 84 over a five year period. Looking at the other parameters, the table below tells the story:

	10%	12%	15%	20%
5 Year	496	326	181	84
10 Year	156	74	27	1
15 Year	93	38	14	2
20 Year	26	5	1	0

Although the number of funds that manage to deliver the returns we are looking for is small, the closer in the time frame, the larger the number of funds meeting those targets. For example, the number of mutual funds making 10% or better returns in the last year is 1544, just under a quarter of all funds. Remember too that the funds in our table weathered the severe market downturn of 2000-2002 and still showed these solid results.

If the government chooses to invest in funds with an average of 15% return in each of the one year, three year and five year time frames, switching as the qualifying funds change, they could easily average between 15% and 20% a year return. By showing such returns in each of those time frames, the respective fund managers show, not only talent, but consistency.

Perhaps an even better route would be for the government to form an administrative board for its nest egg comprised of the lead investment managers for each of the qualifying funds. Or it could form a panel of expert advisors based on the longer term best performing funds.

And there is no need to stay invested in Canada. The nest egg fund could invest globally...and let the success of businesses in other countries pay for our government.

While I believe 15% a year return is achievable, 10% a year certainly is. And an annual return fluctuating between 10% and higher is the most likely scenario.

There is a caveat here. There should be limits on how much of a particular company the nest egg fund could buy, probably the same limits as apply to any other mutual fund. Also, the nest egg fund's involvement with companies it has an interest in should be arm's length. The fund should not be involved in the day to day management and operations of companies it invests in nor should it try to get representatives on corporate boards of directors. The nest egg fund should not be used as a vehicle for nationalizing businesses.

What's the Real Upside Here?

Once the personal income tax has been eliminated, the government can do the whole thing again with the corporate income tax and eventually with all the sources of government revenue. Even the amount of the budget given to reducing the national debt would be self-financed. The debt would be eliminated automatically.

But what's the real upside here? Merely a lighter financial load for we weary taxpayers? (Or at least the grandchildren of we weary taxpayers!) No! Hardly.

The level of taxation affects the economy. It affects the attraction of foreign investment. It affects entrepreneurship and new business growth. As a tax free country, and not just some tax free tiny little oil fiefdom but a major country with the second largest land area in the world and one of the richest troves of minerals in the world, Canada would become a magnet for investment, entrepreneurship and the creation of wealth. Canada could become like Hong Kong in its heyday, an economic powerhouse, but with our greater resources, we would make Hong Kong look like a pussy cat.

Canada could be at the forefront of science, business, and the arts. It could become the most important economic power in the world. Or at least running a close second to China if it continues to grow into an economic power to be reckoned with.

Certainly, Canada would eventually outstrip the United States in economic power if the U.S. continues to debauch its currency and spend itself into the poorhouse through its imperialist adventures. Canada - no taxes, no debt. United States - taxes, ballooning debt. The United States will suffer a brain drain as its best minds emigrate to Canada.

This idea, this paradigm shift in the way we look at the financing of government, is an idea whose time has come. Write the Prime Minister! Write your member of parliament. Let's make this happen. If not for ourselves, for our children and our grandchildren and the future of this great country.

HOW TO MOVE TO CANADA

Greenland
(DK)
Alaska
(US)
Yukon
North-
west
Territories
Nunavut
Newfoundland
British
Columbia
Alberta
Saskat-
chewan
Manitoba
Québec
PEI
Ontario
Nova
Scotia
New
Brunswick
United States

Chapter 6

Immigrating to Canada

Coming to Canada as an immigrant is an exciting opportunity. However, there are several things you should consider before you apply to be a permanent resident.

In most cases, you must apply at a Canadian visa office outside of Canada. In some cases, you can apply to become a permanent resident after you arrive in Canada. For example, live-in caregivers or people granted refugee protection can apply from within Canada.

If you want to immigrate to Canada, there are a few different ways to apply. You will need to decide which immigration program will work best for you and your family.

Find out about the requirements and the steps to apply in each category:

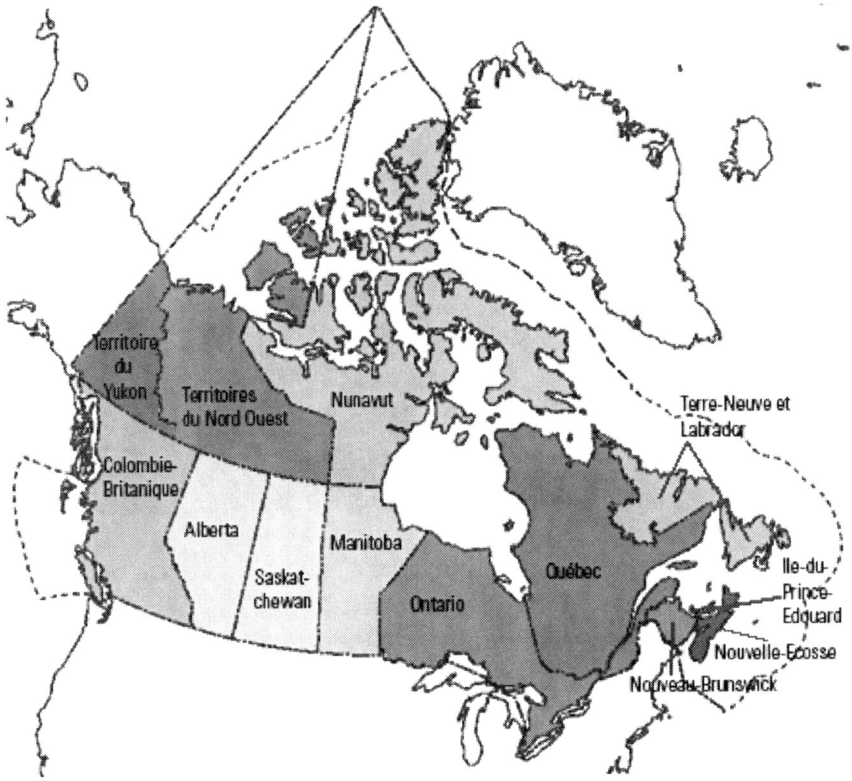

Skilled Workers And Professionals

Skilled workers have education, work experience, knowledge of English or French, and other abilities that will help them to establish themselves successfully as permanent residents in Canada.

Making an application to immigrate to Canada is straightforward. This section will help you to find guides, information and the forms you need to make your application.

The rules for applying as a skilled worker can change from time to time, so make sure you visit this site regularly if you are considering immigrating to Canada as a skilled worker.

Before you apply, make sure you refer to updated selection criteria, and are familiar with the current application procedures. After you apply, make sure you return to this web page to find out about the steps that follow.

Note: You must meet the following minimum requirements to apply as a skilled worker:

- You have at least one continuous year of full-time, paid work experience or the equivalent in part-time continuous employment.
- Your work experience must be Skill Type 0 (managerial occupations) or Skill Level A (professional occupations) or B (technical occupations and skilled trades) on the Canadian National Occupational Classification (NOC).
- You must have had this experience within the last 10 years.

Frequently Asked Questions: Skilled Workers And Professionals

Simplified application process

Why has Citizienship and Immigration Canada introduced the simplified application process for Federal Economic Class applications?

Citizienship and Immigration Canada (CIC) is committed to client-focused service delivery. CIC recognized that changes in procedure could simplify the initial application requirements for Federal Economic Class applicants waiting to have their applications assessed.

When did the simplified application process come into effect?

The simplified application process came into effect on September 1, 2006.

What does the simplified application process involve?

Simplified kits and forms have been developed to guide applicants through the application process. Applicants are required to complete and submit a three-page form along with the processing fees, which secures them a place in the processing line.

All supporting documents will be requested at a later date, usually about four months before the visa office is ready to assess the application. A letter of receipt provides advice to the applicant on labour-market preparation. The letter also encourages applicants to take advantage of the waiting period. For example, some applicants could use this time to start courses to improve their language skills.

What does the supporting documentation to be provided later include?

Supporting documentation would include education documents or other certificates attesting to the educational level, employment letters confirming work experience, language test results, police certificates, birth and marriage certificates, and bank statements confirming the applicant's funds.

Is the simplified application process being used at all visa offices?

Since September 1, 2006, the simplified application process is in use at all visa offices except Buffalo, U.S.A. For applicants who submit their applications in Buffalo for processing by Buffalo and the other U.S. offices, the regular application process continues to apply. Applicants must submit their supporting documents at the same time as the application form.

Why is the simplified application process not being used by Buffalo and other U.S. offices?

Buffalo and its partner missions in the U.S. use a streamlined system where all files are created and pre-processed in Buffalo. It requires you to submit all relevant documents and information with your application. This makes processing faster for most clients who already live in Canada or the U.S. The SAP does not work well with this system.

Can a foreigner living in the United States who has legal status submit a simplified application?

No. Since Buffalo continues to use the regular application process, American citizens and other residents of the United States must submit a full application to our visa office in Buffalo, which will then forward it to the visa office closest to the applicant's residence.

If you submit a simplified application to Buffalo, it will be returned to you with a letter requesting you submit a regular application. Any fees sent with the simplified application will also be returned.

If I am using the simplified application process, do I have to notify the visa office if I change jobs?

No. You only have to notify the visa office if you have a new address (postal or email) or hire a new immigration representative.

You should also contact the visa office if you decide to withdraw your application. You do not have to notify Citizenship and Immigration Canada of any other changes until the visa office contacts you (about four months before the office is ready to assess your application).

I have already submitted my application. Do I have to start over?

No. Applications that were submitted before September 1, 2006, will be processed as usual. Regular applications received after September 1, 2006, are accepted, but the supporting documents will be returned to the applicant until the visa office requests them.

Why do you return the supporting documents?

The simplified process is intended to help applicants by eliminating the burden of continuously having to submit documents while waiting for their application to be processed. It also allows Citizienship and Immigration Canada to avoid duplication of work and save storage space. In addition, given application processing times, most documents would have to be updated if the applicant's situation changes (for example, marital status, job, education and financial situation).

I have been nominated under a province's immigration program. Do I submit a simplified application?

No. Individuals applying under a provincial nomination program do not submit a simplified application because these applications are processed on a priority basis.

Will my processing fees be refunded if I decide to withdraw my application?

Yes. If you contact the visa office before they contact you (that is, before the assessment of your application begins), your fees will be refunded.

I LOVE CANADA

Will this initiative reduce processing times?

No. However, the simplified application process will reduce the amount of information you need to submit when you apply. It also secures you a place in the processing line, and you won't have to submit supporting documents more than once.

I have just taken a language proficiency test at a designated organization, such as the International English Language Testing System (IELTS), Canadian English Language Proficiency Index Program (CELPIP) or the Test d'évaluation de français (TEF). Can I submit the results now?

If you apply under the simplified application process, the visa office will not accept any supporting documents. If you submit documents with your application, they will be returned to you.

Submit your language test results with your other supporting documents. The visa office will contact you to request these documents about four months before your application is processed. If you take the language test within one year of submitting your simplified application, the results remain valid and will be accepted as supporting documentation by the visa office.

Investors, Entrepreneurs And Self-Employed Persons

The Business Immigration Program seeks to attract experienced business people to Canada who will support the development of a strong and prosperous Canadian economy.

Business immigrants are expected to make a C$400,000 investment or to own and manage businesses in Canada.

Canada has three classes of business immigrants:

- investors

- entrepreneurs and
- self-employed persons.

Each application can be made for only one class and cannot be changed once the application is submitted. The criteria you must meet to qualify are different for each class.

Find out if you can immigrate as one of the following:

Investors

The Immigrant Investor Program seeks to attract experienced business people to invest C$400,000 into Canada's economy. Investors must:

- show that they have business experience
- have a minimum net worth of C$800,000 that was obtained legally and
- make a C$400,000 investment.

Your investment is managed by Citizenship and Immigration Canada (CIC) and is guaranteed by the Canadian provinces that use it to create jobs and help their economies grow.

CIC will return your C$400,000 investment, without interest, about five years and two months after payment.

Entrepreneurs

The Entrepreneur Program seeks to attract experienced business persons who will own and actively manage businesses in Canada that contribute to the economy and create jobs. Entrepreneurs must:

- show that they have business experience
- have a minimum net worth of C$300,000 that was obtained legally and
- respect the conditions for entrepreneurs after they arrive in Canada.

Self-Employed Persons

The Self-Employed Persons Program seeks to attract applicants who have the intention and ability to become self-employed in Canada. Self-employed persons are required to have either:

- relevant experience that will make a significant contribution to the cultural or athletic life of Canada or
- experience in farm management and the intention and ability to purchase and manage a farm in Canada.

Chapter 7

Frequently Asked Questions: Investors, Entrepreneurs And Self-Employed Persons

Investors

What are the requirements for qualifying as an investor?

To qualify as an investor, you must have two years of business experience and a net worth of at least C$800,000 that was obtained legally. You must also obtain a minimum of 35 points in a selection grid designed to determine whether you will be able to become economically established in Canada. Before a visa is issued, you must make an investment of C$400,000 to Citizenship and Immigration Canada.

You can find more information on the Immigrant Investor Program, including definitions of the various terms that apply to the Program, in the Related Links section at the bottom of this page.

What is the procedure for becoming an investor?

You must meet all the eligibility requirements, pass medical, criminal and security checks, and make an investment of C$400,000. You can find more information under *How to apply* in the Related Links section at the bottom of this page.

What are the business experience requirements?

You must have been a part or full owner of a business for two years or more, or have managed the equivalent of five full-time workers in a business for a minimum of two full years. You will find full details in the Related Links section at the bottom of this page.

Does the business experience have to be recent?

The business experience must be in the period that begins five years before you submit your application and ends when a decision is made on your application.

What is meant by "business"?

You can find definitions of all the terms that apply to the Immigrant Investor Program in the Related Links section at the bottom of this page.

How do I satisfy Citizenship and Immigration Canada that my net worth was obtained legally?

You must be able to prove that no portion of your net worth was obtained through criminal activity. You will be asked to explain any discrepancies between your net income over the years and your present net worth. The visa officer who assesses your net worth may ask you for documents to back up both your income sources and your net worth.

Who is responsible for the investment operations of the program?

Citizenship and Immigration Canada (CIC) administers all aspects of the program, including the investment that successful applicants must make. CIC acts as an agent for the participating provinces and territories.

What documents do I receive after I make my investment?

You will receive a zero interest promissory note that is not transferable. You cannot sell the promissory note, but you can use it as collateral for a loan. At the maturity date, you must return the promissory note to Citizenship and Immigration Canada for repayment of your C$400,000 investment.

Why do you recommend that I make my investment through a Citizenship and Immigration Canada-approved facilitator?

Citizenship and Immigration Canada has set up administrative procedures with a number of facilitators to assist in the payment and redemption of your C$400,000 investment. These services are available to you at no cost. Facilitators also offer a variety of financing options if you want to finance your investment or use your promissory note as collateral for a loan in the future. You can find more information about facilitators in the Related Links section at the bottom of this page.

Where do most immigrant investors come from?

Investors come from all over the world. Currently, the majority of investors are from China, Taiwan, Korea and Hong Kong, but there are also substantial numbers of investors applying from the Middle East and elsewhere. You can find more information on where business immigrants come from in Citizenship and Immigration Canada's annual report, *Facts and Figures*. You will find a link to the report in the Related Links section at the bottom of this page.

Investors: Definitions

In order to qualify, you must first meet the definition of an investor. The following terms are defined in the regulations:

Investor means a foreign national who

1. has business experience;
2. has a legally obtained net worth of at least CAN $800,000; and
3. indicates in writing to an officer that they intend to make or have made an investment.

Business experience in respect of

1. an investor, other than an investor selected by a province, means a minimum of two years of experience consisting of
    1. two one-year periods of experience in the management of a qualifying business and the control

of a percentage of equity of the qualifying business during the period beginning five years before the date of application for a permanent resident visa and ending on the day a decision is made on the application; or

2. two one-year periods of experience in the management of at least five full-time job equivalents per year in a business during the period beginning five years before the date of application for a permanent resident visa and ending on the day a decision is made on the application, or
3. a combination of a one-year period of experience described in subparagraph (i) and a one-year period of experience described in subparagraph (ii);

Full-time job equivalent means 1,950 hours of paid employment.

Minimum net worth means that the investor must have at least $800,000 to qualify as an Immigrant Investor.

Net assets, in respect of a qualifying business or a qualifying Canadian business, means the assets of the business, minus the liabilities of the business, plus shareholder loans made to the business by the foreign national who is making or has made an application for a permanent resident visa and their spouse or common-law partner.

Net income, in respect of a qualifying business or a qualifying Canadian business, means the after tax profit or loss of the business plus remuneration by the business to the foreign national who is making or has made an application for a permanent resident visa and their spouse or common-law partner.

Net worth, in respect of an investor, other than an investor selected by a province, means the fair market value of all of the assets of the investor and their spouse or common-law partner minus the fair market value of all of their liabilities;

Percentage of equity means

1. in respect of a sole proprietorship, 100 per cent of the equity of the sole proprietorship controlled by a foreign national or their spouse or common-law partner;
2. in respect of a corporation, the percentage of the issued and outstanding voting shares of the capital stock of the corporation controlled by a foreign national or their spouse or common-law partner; and
3. in respect of a partnership or joint venture, the percentage of the profit or loss of the partnership or joint venture to which a foreign national or their spouse or common-law partner is entitled.

Qualifying business means a business—other than a business operated primarily for the purpose of deriving investment income such as interest, dividends or capital gains—for which, during the year under consideration, there is documentary evidence of any two of the following:

1. the percentage of equity multiplied by the number of full-time job equivalents is equal to or greater than two full-time job equivalents per year;
2. the percentage of equity multiplied by the total annual sales is equal to or greater than $500,000;
3. the percentage of equity multiplied by the net income in the year is equal to or greater than $50,000; and
4. the percentage of equity multiplied by the net assets at the end of the year is equal to or greater than $125,000.

Chapter 9

Frequently Asked Questions: Investors, Entrepreneurs And Self-Employed Persons

Entrepreneurs

What are the requirements for qualifying as an entrepreneur?

To qualify as an entrepreneur, you must have at least two years of business experience and a net worth of at least C$300,000 that was obtained legally. You must also obtain a minimum of 35 points in a selection grid designed to determine whether you will be able to become economically established in Canada.

You must also make a commitment to own and operate a business in Canada that will contribute to the economy and create jobs. After you become a permanent resident in Canada, you will have three years to meet the conditions of the Entrepreneur Class.

What is the procedure to become an entrepreneur?

You must meet the definition of an entrepreneur, pass medical, criminal and security checks, and agree to operate a business in Canada. You can find more information under *How to apply* in the Related Links section at the bottom of this page.

What are the business experience requirements?

You can meet the business experience requirements if you have owned a percentage of a business of a specified size for at least two full years. Please consult the definition of an entrepreneur for more details in the Related Links section at the bottom of this page.

Does the business experience have to be recent?

The business experience must occur within the period that begins five years before you sign your application and ends when a decision is made on your application.

What is meant by "business"?

You can find more information on the Entrepreneur Program, including definitions of the various terms that apply to the Program, in the Related Links section at the bottom of this page.

How do I satisfy Citizenship and Immigration Canada that my net worth was obtained legally?

You will have to satisfy the visa officer that no portion of your net worth was obtained as a result of criminal activity. You should be able to explain material differences between your net income over the years and your present net worth, and to comply with reasonable requests for documents to back up both your income sources and the components of your net worth.

Who do I contact for more information about meeting my business conditions in Canada?

Once you are accepted into the Entrepreneur Program, you will receive a brochure that contains instructions and contact information for the Citizenship and Immigration Canada (CIC) offices in Canada. You are required to contact a CIC office within six months after you enter Canada as a permanent resident to report your address and telephone number. You must provide a further update on your progress 18 months after you arrive in Canada.

Where do most entrepreneurs come from?

Entrepreneurs come from all over the world. Currently, the majority of entrepreneurs are from China, Taiwan, Korea and Hong Kong, but there are also large numbers of them applying from the Middle East and elsewhere.

You can find more information on where business immigrants come from in the annual report, *Facts and Figures* from Citizenship and Immigration Canada. You will find a link to the report in the Related Links section at the bottom of this page.

Entrepreneurs: Definitions

In order to qualify, you must first meet the definition of an entrepreneur. If your application is accepted you must also comply with the conditions for an entrepreneur after arriving in Canada.

The following terms are defined in the regulations:

Entrepreneur means a foreign national who

1. has business experience;
2. has a legally obtained minimum net worth of $300,000; and
3. provides a written statement to an officer that they intend and will be able to meet the conditions listed at the bottom of this page

Business experience in respect of an entrepreneur, means a minimum of two years of experience consisting of two one-year periods of experience in the management of a qualifying business and the control of a percentage of equity of the qualifying business during the period beginning five years before the date of application for a permanent resident visa and ending on the day a decision is made on the application.

Full-time job equivalent means 1,950 hours of paid employment.

Minimum net worth means in respect of an entrepreneur, $300,000.

Net assets, in respect of a qualifying business or a qualifying Canadian business, means the assets of the business, minus the liabilities of the business, plus shareholder loans made to the business by the foreign national who is making or has made an application for a permanent resident visa and their spouse or common-law partner.

Net income, in respect of a qualifying business or a qualifying Canadian business, means the after tax profit or loss of the business plus remuneration by the business to the foreign national who is making or has made an application for a permanent resident visa and their spouse or common-law partner's income.

Net worth, in respect of an entrepreneur, means the fair market value of all of the assets of the entrepreneur and their spouse or common-law partner minus the fair market value of all of their liabilities.

Percentage of equity means

1. in respect of a sole proprietorship, 100 per cent of the equity of the sole proprietorship controlled by a foreign national or their spouse or common-law partner;
2. in respect of a corporation, the percentage of the issued and outstanding voting shares of the capital stock of the corporation controlled by a foreign national or their spouse or common-law partner; and
3. in respect of a partnership or joint venture, the percentage of the profit or loss of the partnership or joint venture to which a foreign national or their spouse or common-law partner is entitled.

Qualifying business means a business—other than a business operated primarily for the purpose of deriving investment income such as interest, dividends or capital gains—for which, during the year under consideration, there is documentary evidence of any two of the following:

1. the percentage of equity multiplied by the number of full-time job equivalents is equal to or greater than two full-time job equivalents per year;
2. the percentage of equity multiplied by the total annual sales is equal to or greater than $500,000;
3. the percentage of equity multiplied by the net income in the year is equal to or greater than $50,000; and
4. the percentage of equity multiplied by the net assets at the end of the year is equal to or greater than $125,000.

Qualifying Canadian business means a business operated in Canada by an entrepreneur—other than a business operated primarily for the purpose of deriving investment income, such as interest, dividends or capital gains—for which there is in any year within the period of three years after the day the entrepreneur becomes a permanent resident documentary evidence of any two of the following:

1. the percentage of equity multiplied by the number of full-time job equivalents is equal to or greater than two full-time job equivalents per year;
2. the percentage of equity multiplied by the total annual sales is equal to or greater than $250,000;
3. the percentage of equity multiplied by the net income in the year is equal to or greater than $25,000; and
4. the percentage of equity multiplied by the net assets at the end of the year is equal to or greater than $125,000.

Conditions

Entrepreneurs must comply with the following conditions:

Permanent residence

An entrepreneur who becomes a permanent resident must meet the following conditions:

1. the entrepreneur must control a percentage of the equity of a qualifying Canadian business equal to or greater than 33 1/3 per cent;
2. the entrepreneur must provide active and on-going management of the qualifying Canadian business; and
3. the entrepreneur must create at least one incremental full-time job equivalent in the qualifying Canadian business for Canadian citizens or permanent residents, other than the entrepreneur and their family members.

Conditions

Note: Quebec has its own business immigration program, and has set different conditions that entrepreneurs must meet. The conditions listed above do not apply to entrepreneurs selected by Quebec. Visit the Quebec Immigration web site for more information on immigrating to Quebec. You will find a link in the *Related Links* section on the bottom of this page.

Applicable time

The entrepreneur must meet the conditions for a period of at least one year within the period of three years after the day on which the entrepreneur becomes a permanent resident.

Evidence of compliance

An entrepreneur who becomes a permanent resident must provide to an officer evidence of compliance with the conditions within the period of three years after the day on which the entrepreneur becomes a permanent resident.

Report and evidence of efforts to comply

An entrepreneur must provide to an officer:

1. not later than six months after the day on which the entrepreneur becomes a permanent resident, their residential address and telephone number; and
2. during the period beginning 18 months after and ending 24 months after the day on which the entrepreneur becomes a permanent resident, evidence of their efforts to comply with the conditions.

Family members

The family members of an entrepreneur are subject to the condition that the entrepreneur meets the conditions set out in this section.

Chapter 10

Self-Employed Persons

What are the requirements for qualifying as a self-employed person?

To qualify as a self-employed person, you must have two years of relevant experience and show that you intend to become self-employed in Canada.

You must also obtain a minimum of 35 points in a selection grid designed to determine whether you will be able to become economically established in Canada.

What is the procedure for becoming a self-employed person?

You must meet the definition of a self-employed person, pass a medical examination, criminal and security checks, and agree to operate a business in Canada. You can find more information under *How to apply* in the Related Links section at the bottom of this page.

What is meant by "relevant experience"?

You can find more information on self-employed persons, including definitions of the various terms that apply to the Program, in the Related Links section at the bottom of this page.

Does the relevant experience have to be recent?

The relevant experience must be in the period that begins five years before you sign your application and ends when a decision is made on your application.

What is meant by "cultural activities"?

"Cultural activities" include occupations generally considered to be part of Canada's artistic and cultural field. Examples include authors and writers, creative and performing artists, musicians, painters, sculptors and other visual artists, technical support and occupations in motion pictures, creative designers and craftspeople. You can find a full list of qualifying activities in the Related Links section at the bottom of this page.

What are specified economic activities?

You must plan to be self-employed in Canada in cultural or athletic activities, or purchase and manage a farm.

What is meant by a "significant contribution"?

There is no formal definition of what constitutes a significant contribution. This gives visa officers the ability to use their judgment and allow them to recognize that a contribution to athletics or the arts, even at less than a national standard, may still be of significant benefit at the local level. For example, a music teacher with reasonable qualifications will be in a better position to make a significant contribution in a small town than in a large city.

Please note that you must contribute to economic activities in Canada. While this does not preclude some activities outside of Canada, your experience must include a significant contribution within Canada.

Are there any reporting requirements once I arrive in Canada?

No. Unlike the Entrepreneur Program, you do not have to meet any conditions after becoming a permanent resident of Canada. However, there are requirements to retain your status as a permanent resident. You can find more information about being a permanent resident under *About permanent resident status* in the Related Links section at the bottom of this page.

Is there a net worth requirement?

There is no regulated minimum net worth requirement. However, you will have to satisfy a visa officer that you have sufficient funds to settle in Canada with your dependants, and to finance the economic activities on which your selection was based. For example, if you are a farmer, you will have to prove that you have sufficient funds to purchase and operate a farm in Canada.

You can find information on the funds that you require in the Related Links section at the bottom of this page.

Self-Employed Persons: Definitions

In order to qualify, you must first meet the definition of a self-employed person. The following terms are defined in the regulations:

Self-employed person means a foreign national who has relevant experience and has the intention and ability to be self-employed in

Canada and to make a significant contribution to specified economic activities in Canada.

Relevant experience in respect of

1. a self-employed person, means a minimum of two years of experience, during the period beginning five years before the date of application for a permanent resident visa and ending on the day a decision is made on the application. The experience must consist of:
    1. in respect of cultural activities,
        1. two one-year periods of experience in self-employment in cultural activities, or
        2. two one-year periods of experience in participation at a world class level in cultural activities, or
        3. a combination of a one-year period of experience described in (A), above, and a one-year period of experience described in (B), above,
    2. in respect of athletics,
        1. two one-year periods of experience in self-employment in athletics, or
        2. two one-year periods of experience in participation at a world class level in athletics, or
        3. a combination of a one-year period of experience described in (A), above, and a one-year period of experience described in (B), above, and
    3. in respect of the purchase and management of a farm, two one-year periods of experience in the management of a farm.

Specified economic activities, in respect of

1. a self-employed person, means cultural activities, athletics or the purchase and management of a farm; and
2. a self-employed person selected by a province, has the meaning provided by the laws of the province.

Chapter 11

FAQ

Business Immigration Program

Why does Canada have a business immigration program?

Canada's Business Immigration Program seeks to attract experienced business people to Canada to support the development of a strong and prosperous Canadian economy. The program includes three classes: the Immigrant Investor Class, the Self-Employed Persons Class and the Entrepreneur Class.

Business immigrants are expected to contribute to the Canadian economy by owning and managing businesses in Canada or by making an investment in the Canadian economy.

What are the principal differences between investors, entrepreneurs and self-employed persons?

Investors must make a C$400,000 investment but are not subject to monitoring or other regulatory requirements once they arrive in Canada.

Entrepreneurs must invest and participate in the management of a business in Canada that creates at least one additional job for someone other than a member of their immediate family. They must report regularly on their progress.

Self-employed persons are selected based on their intention and ability to create a job for themselves in cultural or athletic activities, or to purchase and manage a farm in Canada. They are not subject to monitoring or other regulatory requirements once they arrive in Canada.

What type of documents do I have to submit to support my application?

In addition to the usual documents required to support any application for immigration to Canada, you must provide documents that demonstrate your past business experience, such as:

- financial statements
- corporate and personal income tax returns
- tax assessments
- bank statements
- business licences
- minute books
- letters of reference and
- promotional material.

Where can I get application forms?

Application forms are available under the *Find an application form or guide* button in the Quick Links section on the right-hand side of this page. They are also available at all Canadian visa offices.

Where do I apply?

You must submit your application to the correct visa office. You can submit it to:

- the office that is responsible for the country where you have been living as a permanent resident or a citizen for at least a year or
- a Canadian visa office in the country where you have citizenship.
- How long will it take for my application to be processed?
- The length of time it takes to process your application is different in each visa office. You can check processing times in the Quick Links section on the right-hand side of this page.

2009

—JEUX DU—
CANADA
—GAMES—

BLOG.DR2ooo.COM (C) 2006

I AM.

Chapter 12

GETTING READY -- BEFORE YOU LEAVE FOR CANADA

- **Essential documents**
- **Important documents**
- **What you should know about health care**
- **What you can bring into Canada**
- **Getting ready to look for work**
- **Getting ready if you are a business immigrant**
- **Communities across Canada**
- **The Canadian climate: What to expect and what clothes to bring**
- **Schools and universities**

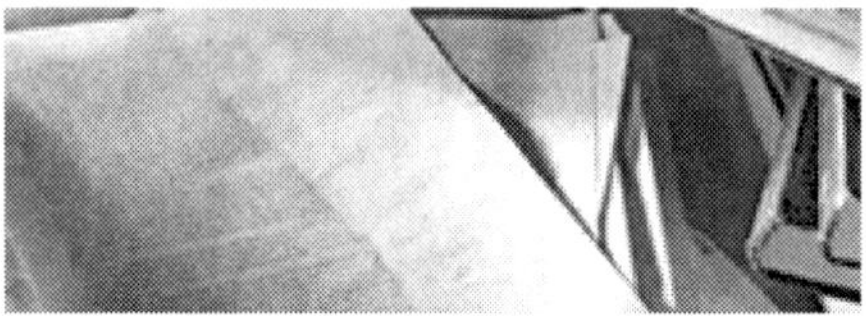

Essential Documents

When you travel to Canada, you will need to have the following documents with you:

- a Canadian immigrant visa and Confirmation of Permanent Residence for each family member travelling with you;

- a valid passport or other travel document for each family member travelling with you;
- two copies of a detailed list of all the personal or household items you are bringing with you; and
- two copies of a list of items that are arriving later.

Note: The lists should state how much your personal and household items are worth.

- You must also bring with you enough money to cover living expenses such as rent, food, clothing and transportation for a six-month period. You may be asked to show proof of your funds.

Do not pack your documents in a suitcase. You will need to have them available to show to immigration and customs officials.

TIP ! Make two copies of these lists -- one for you to keep and one for the Canada Customs officer. You can get the Canada Customs and Revenue Agency form for this purpose from the Internet at www.ccra-adrc.gc.ca/E/pbg/cf/b4abq

Important documents

Depending on your personal situation, you should bring the following important documents with you to Canada:

- birth certificates or baptismal certificates;
- marriage certificates;
- adoption, separation or divorce papers;
- school records, diplomas or degrees for each family member travelling with you;
- trade or professional certificates and licences;
- letters of reference from former employers;

- a list of your educational and professional qualifications and job experience (this is also called a résumé);
- immunization, vaccination, dental and other health records for each family member;
- driver's licence, including an International Driver's Permit, and a reference from your insurance company;
- photocopies of all essential and important documents, in case the originals get lost (be sure to keep the photocopies in a separate place from the originals); and
- car registration documents (if you are importing a motor vehicle into Canada).

TIP ! If possible, get all of your documents translated into English or French by a qualified translator before you leave for Canada.

What You Should Know About Health Care

Canada has a public health-care system known as "medicare." It provides insurance coverage for health-care services to all Canadian citizens and permanent residents. (You will be a "permanent resident.") The federal government sets health-care standards for the whole country, but the programs are run by the provincial ministries of health. More information on the health-care system can be found in *Your first few days in Canada*.

> **TIP !** Apply for provincial health-care coverage as soon as possible after you arrive in the province where you plan to live.

Note: British Columbia, Ontario, Quebec and New Brunswick have a three-month waiting period before you become eligible for medicare coverage. If you are planning to settle in any of these provinces, you should buy private health insurance coverage for the first three months. Insurance companies are listed in the Yellow Pages of all Canadian telephone books, under "Insurance."

> **TIP !** Bring a supply of your medications with you to allow you time to find a family doctor in Canada from whom you will have to get new prescriptions. (getting insurance before you travel will cost you less)

What You Can Bring Into Canada

There are strict laws about what you can bring into Canada.

Cars must meet Canadian safety and pollution control standards. Many cars are not allowed into the country. Contact Transport Canada for more information before you ship your car.

Transport Canada, Vehicle Importation
330 Sparks Street, Tower C
Ottawa, Ontario K1A 0N5

Telephone: 1 (613) 998-8616
(when calling from outside Canada)

1 800 333-0371
(toll-free, from inside Canada)

Web site: www.tc.gc.ca

(follow the link to Vehicle Importation)

The following items cannot be brought into Canada:

- unauthorized firearms, explosives, fireworks and ammunition;
- narcotics, other than prescription drugs;
- meat, dairy products, fresh fruits and vegetables;
- plants, flowers and soil;
- endangered species of animals or products made from animal parts, such as the skin, feathers, fur, bones and ivory;
- cultural property, including antique and cultural objects considered to have historical significance in their country of origin (you may, however, bring family heirlooms);
- more than 200 cigarettes (you must pay tax on the excess amount) per person over 18 years of age if you are immigrating to Quebec, Alberta, Saskatchewan or Manitoba, or per person over 19 if you are immigrating to Ontario or any of the other provinces; and
- more than 1.5 litres of commercial alcohol (you must pay tax on the excess amount) per person over 19 years of age.

If you are not sure about an item, you can write to or telephone:

Canada Customs and Revenue Agency
Customs, Excise and Taxation
Information Services
2265 St. Laurent Boulevard
Ottawa, Ontario K1G 4K3

Telephone: 1 (506) 636-5064
(when calling from outside Canada)

1 800 461-9999
(toll-free, from inside Canada)

Web site: www.ccra-adrc.gc.ca

Getting Ready To Look For Work

If possible, have your documents translated into English or French before you leave for Canada. Essential documents for looking for work include:

- a résumé of your education, work and volunteer experience, and your skills and qualifications;
- diplomas, degrees, certificates and other qualifications;
- letters of recommendation; and
- school records or transcripts.

> **TIP !** Improving your English or French before coming to Canada would be extremely beneficial.

Research the labour market in the part of Canada where you plan to settle. The following federally funded Web sites will be helpful:

- www.workinfonet.ca**:** This is a national Web site for career and labour market information. It contains job information for each province and territory. It also contains information on self-employment, education and training.
- www.workdestinations.org**:** This Web site contains information on various jobs, working conditions, labour market trends, living conditions, and training and

educational opportunities in different regions of Canada. It also lists regulated jobs in Canada. You can find out whether your job is regulated and what you will need to do to get a licence to practise.

- lmi-imt.hrdc-drhc.gc.ca: This Web site offers labour market information, which can help you search for work and make general employment, training and career decisions.
- workplace.hrdc-drhc.gc.ca/page2.asp?sect=1: This Web site offers links to Canadian newspapers' on-line "Help Wanted" advertisements.
- www.worksitecanada.com/news: This Web site links to the employment section in the classified advertisements pages of Canada's daily newspapers to give you an idea of the jobs available now.

TIP ! Professionals in government-regulated occupations should contact the licensing body in their province of destination. See *Employment in regulated professions and trades*. *(Read Fact Sheet-2)*

TIP ! To be better prepared to look for work in Canada, have your credentials evaluated and compared with the Canadian education system to make it easier for employers to determine whether you meet their job requirements. See *International educational assessment services in Canada*.

Getting Ready If You Are A Business Immigrant

If you are coming to Canada as a business immigrant, use the Internet to find out about sources of financing, business opportunities, export and investment services, self-employment assistance and information for small businesses. There are many rules for starting a business in Canada. The following Government of Canada Web sites will help you get a head start in your planning:

- www.cbsc.org: The Canada Business Service Centre's Web site is your single point of contact for information on government services, programs and rules for business.
- www.strategis.gc.ca: This Industry Canada Web site has business information to help you find partners, do market research, find new technologies, and learn about financing opportunities and growth areas in the Canadian economy.
- www.bdc.ca: This is the Web site of the Business Development Bank of Canada. It provides financial and consulting services to Canadian small businesses, especially those in the technology and export sectors of the economy. It also offers information on how to start a business and make it succeed.
- http://strategis.ic.gc.ca/sc_mangb/smallbus/engdoc/sbla.html : This is the Web site of the Canada Small Business Financing Program. The program can help you finance your own business.

- www.contractscanada.gc.ca: This Web site has information on how and what the Government of Canada buys (both goods and services).
- www.cic.gc.ca: This is the Web site of Citizenship and Immigration Canada. It describes the Business Immigration Program. You will find many answers to your questions at this site.

> **TIP !** When you are deciding how much money to bring into Canada, it helps to research the cost of living in the part of Canada where you plan to live. This information can be found on the provincial and territorial Web sites at canada.gc.ca/othergov/prov_e.html.

Communities Across Canada

Most newcomers to Canada tend to settle in the three biggest cities - Toronto, Montréal and Vancouver. But many newcomers and many Canadians choose to live in the medium-sized cities, which they feel have as much to offer as the larger cities with a better quality of life.

Among the medium-sized cities are Halifax, Québec City, Ottawa, London, Windsor, Sudbury, Winnipeg, Saskatoon, Regina, Calgary and Edmonton.

> **TIP !** To locate the medium-sized cities on a map of Canada, go to *Map of Canada*.

All of the medium-sized cities have diverse, multi-ethnic populations ranging in size from approximately 100,000 to one million people, and all have the variety of public and private institutions and services found in the largest cities.

Some newcomers like the idea of living in smaller cities or towns like Moncton, Fredericton and Victoria, or prefer to live in a rural area. Depending on your skills or professional qualifications, some regions may have better job opportunities than others.

> **TIP !** Outside the larger cities, the costs of housing, higher education and services are often much lower.

If you use the Internet, visit the Web sites of each province and territory to see what each has to offer. To find these Web sites, visit canada.gc.ca/othergov/prov_e.html.

Each Web site has a list of government departments and agencies. In the bigger provinces, some government departments may have their own Web sites, with more detailed information. You may also find a directory of on-line services, a link to educational institutions, and a link to major cities and towns. Most of the Web sites also have a tourism section, where you can discover the special attractions of each province and territory.

As mentioned earlier in this chapter, the Web site www.workdestinations.org has links to information on the labour market and the housing market of communities across Canada. It also has useful tips and information about moving within Canada.

You can also visit a Web site called Canadian Government Information on the Internet at www.cgii.gc.ca. It is another useful link to federal, provincial and municipal government information.

TIP ! Most Web sites have a search engine. When you click on the search button, you can look for specific information on immigration, multiculturalism, citizenship, education, training, employment, housing, labour, health, employment opportunities or jobs by typing in these key words.

TIP ! Research carefully the labour market trends or access to your profession in the province and city where you wish to live.

The Canadian Climate: What To Expect And What Clothes To Bring

Most of Canada has four distinct seasons: spring, summer, autumn and winter. The temperatures and weather in each season can be different from one part of the country to another. Here is what you can expect:

Spring: Spring is a rainy season in most parts of Canada. Daytime temperatures rise steadily, but the nights remain cool. Average daytime temperatures are about 12°C in March, April and early May.

Summer: Summer officially begins on June 21, but July and August are summer for most Canadians. In summer, the weather is very warm in most parts of the country. In southern Canada, daytime temperatures are normally above 20°C and can sometimes rise above 30°C.

Autumn: The autumn season, or fall, as it's often called, begins in September. The weather cools and the leaves on many trees change colour and fall to the ground. It can also be very rainy at this time of year. In some parts of Canada, especially northern or mountain regions, snow may begin to fall by late October. Average daytime temperatures are about 10°C to 12°C in most of the country. The autumn months are September, October and November.

Winter: During the winter months (December, January and February), the temperature in most of the country usually stays below 0°C, day and night. Temperatures in some parts of the country periodically drop below -25°C, while along the West Coast, the temperature rarely drops below 0°C. In most of Canada, snow will be on the ground from mid-December to the middle of March. The higher in elevation and the farther north you go, the longer and colder winter becomes.

> **TIP !** You can find detailed weather information for each region of Canada on the Environment Canada Web site: weatheroffice.ec.gc.ca.

> **TIP !** If you arrive in Canada in the winter, you will need warm clothing such as insulated, waterproof boots; an overcoat; a scarf for your neck; a hat that covers your ears; and gloves or mittens. If you come from a warm climate, buy some winter clothes before you leave for Canada, if possible. Or, be ready to buy winter clothes soon after arriving (note also that winter clothes are more expensive than summer clothes). You may wish to contact an immigrant-serving organization in your new community for help.

Schools And Universities

There is no national school system in Canada. Schools and universities are run by the provinces; therefore, education varies somewhat from province to province. Most elementary and secondary schooling is public, meaning it is free and open to everyone.

Depending on the individual province, primary education starts at pre-kindergarten and continues to the end of grade 6 or 8. This is followed by secondary education or high school. In some provinces this may be divided into junior high (grades 7 to 9) and senior high (grades 10 to 12). Normally, students must complete the required academic courses in high school in order to be admitted to university or college.

The regular school year runs from late August or early September until mid- to late June. New students can usually be registered throughout the school year. Most schools are closed on national holidays. Also, all schools are closed between Christmas Eve and New Year's Day, and most are closed for a week in March for spring break. The longest school holiday occurs over the summer months of July and August.

Universities and community colleges hold their regular classes from late August or early September until April, although some courses are offered from January to April and a smaller number are available over the summer months. University and community college courses are not free and the costs vary among the provinces.

When you register your children at the local school or school board

> **TIP !** Education in Canada is available in English and French. Many Canadian parents, even if they do not speak French themselves, believe it is good for their children to be able to speak both English and French. Some put their children in a
>
> French immersion program, where children learn most of the regular subjects in French.

office, you must take with you:

- Canadian immigrant visa (Record of Landing);
- birth certificate or baptismal certificate;
- vaccination certificate;
- any previous school records.

Your children's language and mathematical skills will be assessed, if necessary, and they will be placed in the program the school thinks is best for them.

> **TIP !** For information about the educational system in Canada, visit the provincial or territorial Web sites at canada.gc.ca/othergov/prov_e.html, or visit ceris.schoolnet.ca/e/, www.aucc.ca or www.accc.ca.

Chapter 13

THE DAY YOU ARRIVE IN CANADA

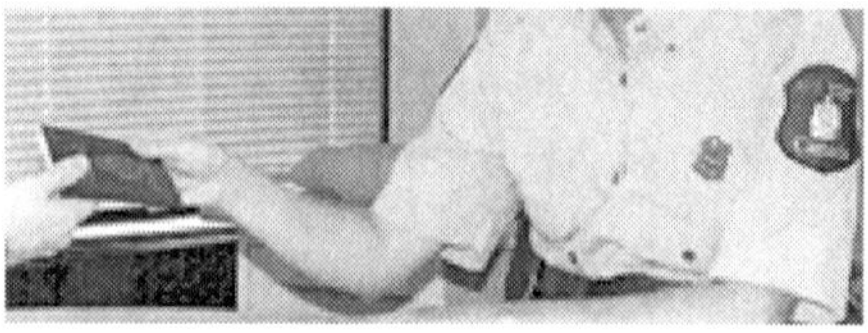

- **Customs and immigration**
- **Reception services**

Customs and immigration

You will probably find the entry procedure fairly straightforward because you have a passport and other essential documents.

You will be interviewed by a Canada Customs officer. You will need to give the officer a list of all the household and personal items that you will be bringing into Canada. You should also show the immigrant visa to the customs officer, who will refer you to an immigration officer.

The immigration officer will check your visa and travel documents and ask you questions similar to those on the Immigrant Application Form, to verify that you are of good character and in good health. At this time, you may also be asked to show proof of your funds. If there are no difficulties, the officer will authorize your entry to Canada as a permanent resident by signing your Record of Landing or Confirmation of Permanent Residence.

If you arrive at one of the major Canadian airports, you will get a booklet called *Welcome to Canada: What You Should Know*. It has information on most aspects of life in Canada. It also provides addresses and telephone numbers for:

- immigrant-serving organizations across Canada;
- language training assessment centres (which help eligible adult newcomers find free language classes);
- useful federal and provincial government offices.

Reception Services

If you arrive in Toronto, Montréal or Vancouver, you will find immigrant reception services in the airport. These services are run by immigrant-serving organizations. They help newcomers get the information and services they need, and this help is often available in several languages. In Montréal, the *Ministère des Relations avec les citoyens et de l'Immigration* runs this service.

> **TIP !** *Welcome to Canada: What You Should Know* and other useful information for newcomers can be found on the Internet at www.cic.gc.ca/english/newcomer, and at www.directioncanada.gc.ca

IMMIGRANT-SERVING ORGANIZATIONS

- **LINC (Language Instruction for Newcomers to Canada)**
- **Host Program**

There are hundreds of immigrant-serving organizations in Canada. Many are staffed by former newcomers to Canada, who understand the challenges that immigrants may face. They usually have people available who speak your language and can accompany you as interpreters. Citizenship and Immigration Canada supports many of these organizations financially, helping newcomers adapt to life in Canada.

Settling in will be much easier if you contact an immigrant-serving organization as soon as you arrive. The people who work for these organizations can help you find a place to live and can answer your questions about shopping, education for your children, transportation, language training and other important matters.

Immigrant-serving organizations can help you:

- find a place to live;
- get your Social Insurance Number and health-care card;
- enroll your children in school;
- get language training;
- find a family doctor;

- find out about government and community services for newcomers;
- look for a job;
- develop a realistic budget; and
- get emergency food aid, if it is needed.

Note: In Quebec, the *Ministère des Relations avec les citoyens et de l'Immigration* is organized into different regions. Each region has a local office, called a *Carrefour d'intégration,* which works with the immigrant-serving organizations to help newcomers adapt to life in Quebec.

Most immigrant-serving organizations offer, or can provide information on, the following Government of Canada programs:

LINC (Language Instruction for Newcomers to Canada)

LINC is a federal government program for all eligible adult immigrants. It offers:

- free language training for adult newcomers who want or need basic English or French;
- language classes given by school boards, colleges and local organizations;
- the choice of studying part time, full time, evenings or weekends, depending on your needs and your schedule; and
- transportation and child-minding, if necessary.

> **TIP !** Your local immigrant-serving organization can direct you to a LINC Assessment Centre, which will then refer you to organizations offering LINC classes. You can also refer to the book Welcome to Canada: What You Should Know to find a LINC Assessment Centre in your area.

Host Program

The Host Program is a federally funded program that matches newcomers with a Canadian family or individual. Host volunteers help you:

- overcome the stress of moving to a new country;
- learn about available services and how to use them;
- practise English or French;
- prepare to look for a job; and
- participate in community activities.

TIP ! Your local immigrant-serving organization can direct you to a Host Program organization in your community.

Immigrant-serving organizations are prepared to help newcomers as soon as they arrive in Canada. These organizations can:

- refer you to economic, social, health, cultural, educational and recreational services;
- give you tips on banking, shopping, managing a household and other everyday tasks;
- provide interpreters or translators, if you need them;
- provide non-therapeutic counselling; and

- help you prepare a professional-looking résumé and learn job-searching skills.

The Immigrant Settlement and Adaptation Program (ISAP), a federal government program, pays for these services.

A list of immigrant-serving organizations across Canada can be found on the Internet at www.cic.gc.ca/english/newcomer/welcome/wel-20e.html

> **TIP !** Manitoba, British Columbia and Quebec have programs similar to LINC, the Host Program and ISAP, but they may have slightly different names.

Chapter 14

YOUR FIRST FEW DAYS IN CANADA

- Finding a place to live
- To buy or to rent
- Types of housing
- How to find a place to live
- What if you have a large family?
- How much will it cost?
- Signing a lease
- Applying for a health-insurance card
- Applying for a Social Insurance Number

Finding A Place To Live
To Buy or To Rent

When you first arrive in Canada, you will probably be living in a temporary home. You will soon be looking for a more permanent place to live. Canada has many different types of housing and a wide range of prices. Finding the right place will take some time and effort. Your first decision will be whether to rent a house or an apartment, or to buy a house.

Whether you rent or buy will depend on your personal finances and whether you already have a job in Canada. Most newcomers decide they should first rent a house or apartment. This gives them more time to save money to buy a house and to decide where they want to live.

If you want to buy a house, unless you can pay the full price, you will need to get a long-term loan called a mortgage. Mortgage loans are provided by banks and other financial institutions. They decide whether the borrower has enough income, more assets than debts, and a good credit rating. Most will ask you to pay at least 10 percent of the cost of the house from your own money.

Types of housing

- **Furnished or unfurnished:** Furnished housing should include beds, tables, chairs, lamps, curtains, a stove and a refrigerator. Unfurnished housing may include a stove and a refrigerator, but not always.
- **Room for rent:** This is usually in a house or an apartment that is owned or rented by other people. Everyone shares the kitchen and bathrooms.
- **Bachelor or studio apartment:** These are small apartments designed mainly for one person. They have one large room with a kitchen and a sleeping area, plus a separate bathroom.
- **Other apartments:** Most other apartments have from one to three bedrooms. All will have a separate kitchen, a living room and a bathroom.
- **Duplex:** This is a house divided into two separate apartments. It may be bought or rented.

- **Townhouse:** This is a small house joined to other houses. It may be bought or rented.
- **Condominium:** This is an apartment or townhouse that is individually owned, while "common areas" are jointly owned. As well as the mortgage payment and property taxes, each owner pays a monthly fee for maintenance, such as snow removal, grass cutting and repairs.

How To Find A Place To Live

Here's how to look for the right home for you:

- search the classified advertisements in local newspapers;
- become familiar with the public transportation available;
- ask an immigrant-serving organization in your area for advice;
- ask friends and family already living in the area for advice;
- look for "Vacancy" or "For Rent" signs on houses and apartment buildings;
- check bulletin boards in grocery stores, Laundromats, health clinics and community centres; and
- ask for advice at your place of worship.

What if you have a large family?

If you have three or more children, or you have older relatives living with you, you will probably not be able to find a big enough apartment. In that case, you may need to think about renting a house.

How much will it cost?

You could expect to pay between $350 a month for a room, and $2,000 a month for a luxury apartment or a large house. Rental costs vary greatly across cities and across Canada. Housing is more reasonable outside the large cities. An immigrant-serving organization in the area where you plan to settle can help you find affordable housing.

Signing a lease

Once you agree to rent an apartment or a house, you may be asked to sign a one-year lease. This legal document of one or two pages describes the rental property, the utilities included and the options, such as parking and storage. It may also state whether pets or more people are allowed. Most apartments are leased by the year, although some are rented monthly.

You will probably need to pay the first and last month's rent when you sign the lease.

> **TIP !** As people in Canada tend to move in the spring and summer months, these are the best times to look for a home; there will be more choices available.

If your apartment requires a lease, your landlord will give you the lease form to sign. Read it over carefully before you sign it. Pay special attention to the parts that state exceptions and additions. You should know which utilities you will pay for and which ones will be paid for by the landlord. Be sure you know what the monthly rent payment includes. For example, is the electricity included? the water included? the parking included?

Also find out whether you have to pay a fee if you leave before the lease term is over. You cannot usually break a lease agreement. It is also likely you will be asked to provide a Canadian reference or to have a co-signer sign the lease to guarantee your financial commitment.

If you don't understand some of the legal terms used in the lease document, contact one of the groups that help immigrants, or someone you know and trust who can help you. Once you sign the lease, it is a legal document.

> **TIP !** Plan on spending 35 to 50 percent of your income on housing. This should include the cost of electricity, heating, telephone service and water. To find out more before you arrive in Canada, visit the Web site www.cic.gc.ca or www.cmhc-schl.gc.ca/en/bureho/reho

Applying For A Health Insurance Card

One of the most important things you need to do as soon as you arrive in Canada is to apply for a health insurance card. All members of your family, even newborn babies, must have their own card. You can get an application form from the provincial ministry of health office, any doctor's office, a hospital or a pharmacy. If necessary, the immigrant-serving organization in your area can help you fill out the form. To apply for a health card, you will need your birth certificate, Record of Landing (IMM 1000) or Confirmation of Permanent Residence (IMM 5292) or PR Card and passport. The Permanent Residence card may also be presented. In most provinces, you will receive coverage as soon as you apply.

> **TIP !** In Ontario, British Columbia, New Brunswick and Quebec, there is a three-month waiting period before you become eligible for medicare coverage. If you are immigrating to any of these provinces, you should get private, short-term health-care insurance for the first three months. Insurance companies are listed in the Yellow Pages of all Canadian telephone books, under "Insurance."

Health-care services covered by medicare include:

- examination and treatment by family doctors;
- many types of surgery;
- most treatment by specialists;
- hospital care;
- X-rays;

- many laboratory tests; and
- most immunizations.

Health-care services not covered by medicare, and for which you will have to pay, include:

- ambulance services;
- prescription drugs;
- dental care; and
- glasses and contact lenses.

These services are sometimes covered by workplace benefit packages.

Your health insurance card is mainly for use in the province where you live. If you are visiting another province and have a medical emergency, you can use your card. However, if you move to another province, you will need to apply for a new card.

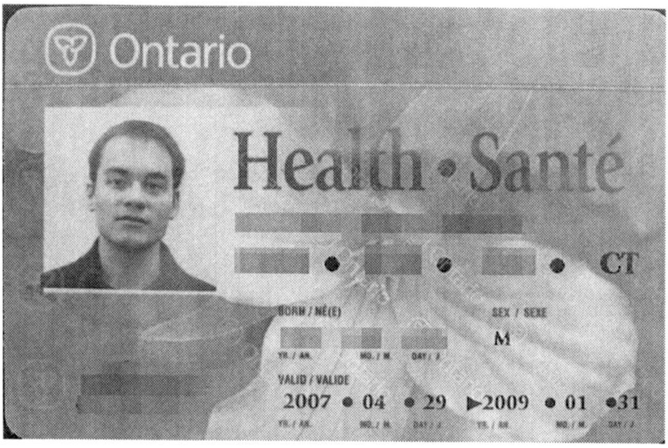

Applying For A Social Insurance Number

To work in Canada, you must have a Social Insurance Number. This is a nine-digit number that you will need to look for a job and to receive government benefits. Sometimes, you will hear people call it the SIN number. You can get a SIN application form through the Human Resources Development Canada Centre near you. These centres are run by the federal government. You can also get a form through your local immigrant-serving organization or from the post office, or you can download one from the Internet at www.hrdc-drhc.gc.ca/sin-nas. The SIN card will be sent to you in the mail. There is a small fee for processing the application.

TIP ! To find the nearest Human Resources Centre, look in the Blue Pages of any telephone book under "Government of Canada -- Employment," or go on the Internet at www.hrdc-drhc.gc.ca/menu/profile-search.shtml#100

Chapter 15

FINDING A JOB, BUILDING A FUTURE

- International educational assessment services in Canada
- Provincial evaluation services
- Employment in regulated professions and trades
- Language skills
- Job opportunities
- Employment laws
- Discrimination
- Deductions and taxable benefits
- Income tax
- Canada Pension Plan
- Employment Insurance
- Taxable benefits
- Union dues

In Canada, full-time jobs are common. However, a growing number of people have part-time or short-term jobs. Women make up a large portion of the work force and many have important, senior positions.

Canadians may change jobs and careers several times. This is often a personal choice. Sometimes people must change jobs because the economy changes. For these, and other reasons, getting a job is not easy. Many people are looking for work.

Newcomers to Canada rarely enter the job market quickly and often must start with jobs below the skill level they worked at in their home country. Once they have Canadian job experience and their ability in English or French improves, so do their job prospects.

International educational assessment services in Canada

Even if you have many years of experience, you do not automatically have the right to practise your trade or profession in Canada. In most cases, you will need to have your credentials assessed to see whether you need more training, education or Canadian work experience before being qualified to practise. You may wish to get your credentials evaluated before you leave for Canada. The following organizations can tell you how to get your credentials assessed:

The Canadian Information Centre for International Credentials Web site (www.cicic.ca) has information on academic and occupational credentials for all of Canada and lists nearly 100 professions and trades, in alphabetical order. When you click on your profession or trade, you will find a link to the address and telephone number of the professional or trade association, the addresses and telephone numbers of provincial evaluation services and regulatory agencies, and labour market information (for example, whether there is a demand for people with your particular trade or profession). You will also be able to find out whether your profession or trade is regulated.

The Centre does not grant equivalencies or assess credentials. It gives advice and refers newcomers to sources of help. To contact the Centre by mail, write to:

Canadian Information Centre for International Credentials

95 St. Clair Avenue West, Suite 1106
Toronto, Ontario M4V 1N6
Telephone: 1 (416) 962-9725
Fax: 1 (416) 962-2800
E-mail: info@cicic.ca
URL: www.cicic.ca

Provincial Evaluation Services

World Education Services assesses academic credentials for a fee. Its assessment will tell you how your education compares with educational standards in the province where you are planning to settle. You can give your assessment to any employer in Canada. It may help you in your job search. To contact World Education Services, write to:

World Education Services Academic Credential Assessment Service
45 Charles Street East, Suite 700
Toronto, Ontario
M4Y 1S2 Canada
Telephone: 1 (416) 972-0070
Toll-free: 1 866 343-0070 (within Canada)
Fax: 1 (416) 972-9004
E-mail: ontario@wes.org
URL: www.wes.org/ca

Education Credentials Evaluation
(Service des équivalences d'études)
Ministère des Relations avec les citoyens
et de l'Immigration
Suite 200
800, De Maisonneuve Boulevard East
Montréal, Quebec
H2L 4L8 Canada
Telephone: 1 (514) 864-9191
Toll-free: 1 877 264-6164 (within Canada)
Fax: 1 (514) 873-8701
E-mail: equivalences@mrci.gouv.qc.ca
URL: www.immq.gouv.qc.ca/equivalences

International Qualifications
Assessment Service
Ministry of Learning
Government of Alberta
4th Floor, Sterling Place
9940-106 Street
Edmonton, Alberta
T5K 2N2 Canada
Telephone: 1 (780) 427-2655
Fax: 1 (780) 422-9734
E-mail: iqas@gov.ab.ca
URL: www.learning.gov.ab.ca/iqas/iqas.asp

International Credential Evaluation Service
4355 Mathissi Place
Burnaby, British Columbia
V5G 4S8 Canada
Telephone: 1 (604) 431-3402
Fax: 1 (604) 431-3382
E-mail: icesinfo@ola.bc.ca
URL: www.ola.bc.ca/ices

Manitoba Credentials Recognition Program
Manitoba Culture, Heritage and Citizenship
Settlement and Labour Market
Services Branch
5th Floor, 213 Notre Dame Avenue
Winnipeg, Manitoba
R3B 1N3 Canada
Telephone: 1 (204) 945-6300 or
1 (204) 945-3162
Fax: 1 (204) 948-2256
E-mail: immigratemanitoba@gov.mb.ca
URL: *www.gov.mb.ca/labour/immigrate/newcomerservices/7c.html*

A proud peace loving Canadian

Employment in Regulated Professions and Trades

In Canada, about 20 percent of jobs are regulated by the government to protect public health and safety. For example, nurses, doctors, engineers, teachers and electricians all work in regulated professions. People who want to work in regulated jobs need to get a licence from the regulatory body in the province in which they live. If you want to know more about how to enter a particular profession or trade in a particular province, you should contact the provincial regulatory body for that job. The professions are self-regulating and they administer the provincial laws that apply to their profession. Rules for entering professions also differ from province to province. (For more information, visit www.cicic.ca.)

> **TIP !** Regulated occupations in Canada usually require many years of education, training and practical experience, and the successful completion of a technical examination. Technical examinations to enter a trade or profession can be very expensive.

Language Skills

It is important to learn English or French as quickly as possible. Many newcomers begin life in Canada by looking for a job that will allow them to learn or improve their English or French. The Language Instruction for Newcomers to Canada (LINC) program gives eligible adult immigrants the chance to take basic English or French classes at no charge.

People with foreign credentials need a Test of English as a Foreign Language (TOEFL) score to enter Canadian colleges and universities. Colleges and universities offering courses in French use various French language tests.

> **TIP !** Look into taking English classes through the LINC Program.

Job Opportunities

- **Human Resources Development Canada Centres:** Counsellors at these centres can give you free advice and information about job and language training and work creation programs for newcomers. They can help you plan an effective job search and prepare a résumé of your education and experience. Each centre also has listings of available jobs on computer or on bulletin boards.

- **Classified advertisements:** Every daily newspaper in Canada has a classified advertisements section where you will find a variety of jobs listed. In many areas, there are also weekly or monthly employment papers that advertise jobs.
- **Local help:** To help newcomers prepare to enter the Canadian work force or to gain access to their profession or trade in Canada, immigrant-serving organizations have a variety of programs. Some give workshops on job search skills, where participants get an overview of the job market where they live. Participants learn, among other things, how to write a good résumé and how to behave in an interview. In some areas, there are job-finding clubs, mentoring programs, programs to help you get volunteer work experience, and wage subsidy programs.

Guess-Who are they ?: Clue: Ask any Sikh (The Kings)

- **Your personal "network":** One of the best ways to learn about jobs is to talk to people. They can be people you know well, or people you have just met. Even if they cannot lead you directly to a job, they can provide you with information, ideas and names of other people who might be able to help and encourage you.

- **The Internet:** Many Web sites have information on job opportunities. You can search for a job on-line in any part of Canada. Some sites also give practical advice on how to plan your job search. Others allow you to apply for a job directly on the Internet, or to post your résumé (in English or French). When you do this, your résumé goes into a database that can be searched by employers. Try visiting the following Web sites, run by the federal government:
- www.hrdc-drhc.gc.ca**:** This is the national Web site of Human Resources Development Canada, a federal department. It is also the gateway to many of the sites mentioned below.
- ele-spe.hrdc-drhc.gc.ca**:** This is an on-line database of jobs and work or business opportunities across Canada. It matches work to people and people to work. You can click on the province where you plan to settle and submit a list of

your skills to the database to find work opportunities that match your profile.

- worksearch.gc.ca: This site will take you through all the steps needed to choose a career and to carry out an effective work search.
- www.workinfonet.ca: This is a national site for career and labour market information. It will link you to job information for each province and territory. It also includes information on self-employment, education and training.
- jb-ge.hrdc-drhc.gc.ca: This is the "Job Bank" Web site. It contains an on-line database of thousands of job vacancies across Canada.
- lmi-imt.hrdc-drhc.gc.ca: This site will link you to detailed labour market information for every city in Canada.
- www.SkillNet.ca: This is a large network of job and career information Web sites. It can link you to full-time and part-time job opportunities.
- www.canadait.com: This site is a gateway to job opportunities in the information technology and communications sector. It has links to company directories and associations that will help you find potential employers.
- www.jobs.gc.ca: This site posts federal government jobs available across the country and accepts on-line applications.
- www.integration-net.cic.gc.ca: This site is run by Citizenship and Immigration Canada. It includes links to many different types of jobs and other useful information for newcomers.

> **TIP** ! When you arrive in Canada, refer to the pamphlet called "Finding Help in Your Community" in the booklet *Welcome to Canada: What You Should Know* for a list of the immigrant-serving organizations across Canada. Contact an agency in your area and ask about job search programs for newcomers.

Employment laws

Federal and provincial laws protect workers and employers by setting minimum wage levels, health and safety standards, and hours of work. They provide for maternity leave, annual paid vacation and protection of children who are working. There are also human rights laws that protect employees from unfair treatment by employers based on sex, age, race, religion or disability.

I love Canadian Employment Laws

Discrimination

There are laws to protect workers from discrimination. For example, an employer must hire employees on the basis of their qualifications. Employers cannot refuse to hire you because they don't like your skin colour or your religion. This is discrimination. It is also discrimination if you are refused a job because of your age, sex, marital status, disability or sexual orientation.

Deductions And Taxable Benefits

Whether you are a Canadian citizen or a permanent resident, when you are hired, your employer will deduct money from your pay cheque to pay for the following:

Income tax

All Canadian residents who are old enough to work must file an income tax return each year, whether they earned any money or not. That is the law. If you are working for an employer, a percentage of your pay cheque will be deducted and sent to the federal government to cover the income tax that you owe. If too much is deducted, you will get a refund. If you paid too little, you will have to pay more. This money helps pay the cost of government services.

Canada Pension Plan

A small part of your pay cheque goes into this plan. When you retire, you will receive a monthly pension from the federal government. The amount will vary according to how many years you worked in Canada before retiring and what your salary was. Residents of Quebec pay into the Quebec Pension Plan, which works the same way as the federal plan. These plans also include survivor's pensions for the spouses of deceased pensioners, disability pensions and death benefits.

Employment Insurance

When you are working, a small percentage of your pay cheque will be deducted each month to go into the Employment Insurance Account. Your employer contributes to the account as well.

Employment Insurance gives money to eligible, unemployed Canadian residents for a short time, while they look for a new job or take some training to learn new skills.

Taxable benefits

Your employer may provide some benefits (for example, life insurance, special medical care, a dental plan or a private pension plan) that are taxable.

Union dues

If you are in a union, and the union has an agreement with your employer, some money will be deducted to pay for the union dues.

What ! if I'm Canadian

I Love My Hockey Team

Canada, the country that could have gotten British culture, French cooking, and American technology, but it ended up with French technology, British cooking, and American culture.

Chapter 16

GENERAL INFORMATION ABOUT CANADA

- Geography
- Distances
- Population
- Map of Canada
- The Francophone population
- History
- Economy
- Government
- Federal government
- Provincial governments
- Territorial governments
- Municipal governments
- Bilingualism
- Multiculturalism
- Protecting the environment -- Sustainable development

Geography

Canada consists of 10 provinces and three territories in five main regions: the Atlantic region, Central Canada, the Prairies, the West Coast and the North. The culture and population are different in each region.

The **Atlantic** region consists of the provinces of Nova Scotia, New Brunswick, Prince Edward Island, and Newfoundland and Labrador. Activities such as fishing, farming, forestry, tourism and mining are important to the Atlantic economy.

Central Canada consists of the provinces of Ontario and Quebec. This is the most populated region of the country. Together, Ontario and Quebec produce more than three-quarters of all Canadian manufactured goods.

The **Prairies** include the provinces of Manitoba, Saskatchewan and Alberta. Much of the land is flat and fertile, excellent for farming and rich in energy resources. In western Alberta, the Prairies end and the Rocky Mountains begin. The Canadian Rockies include some of the largest peaks in North America.

On the **West Coast,** the province of British Columbia is famous for its mountain ranges and forests. Natural resources such as lumber and fish are important to the economy. Fruit farming is also a major industry, as is tourism.

The **North** consists of Canada's three territories: Yukon, the Northwest Territories and Nunavut. Together, they make up over one-third of Canada's land mass. Northern resources include oil, natural gas, gold, lead and zinc.

Distances

Distances in Canada are measured in kilometres. Canada is over 7,000 kilometres from east to west. You would need seven days to drive from Halifax, Nova Scotia, to Vancouver, British Columbia. By airplane, the same trip would take about seven hours.

Population

Canada has about 32 million people. More than 80 percent of all the people in Canada live in towns and cities within 250 kilometres of the United States border. Ottawa is Canada's capital city, with a population of nearly one million. It is located in the province of Ontario. Canada's largest cities are Toronto, Ontario (5.2 million people); Montréal, Quebec (3.6 million); and Vancouver, British Columbia (2.1 million).

Lovely Population

Map of Canada

Region	Province/Territory	Capital
Atlantic Region	Newfoundland and Labrador	St. John's
	Prince Edward Island	Charlottetown
	Nova Scotia	Halifax
	New Brunswick	Fredericton
Central Canada	Quebec	Québec
	Ontario	Toronto
Prairie Provinces	Manitoba	Winnipeg
	Saskatchewan	Regina
	Alberta	Edmonton
West Coast	British Columbia	Victoria
North	Nunavut	Iqaluit
	Northwest Territories	Yellowknife
	Yukon	Whitehorse

Note: *You can view a full size coloured North American map by visiting following link.*
http://www.lonelyplanet.com/mapshells/north_america/canada/canada.htm

The Francophone Population

French is the mother tongue of 6.6 million Canadians. Most Francophones live in Quebec, but almost one million Francophones live in Canada's other provinces and territories. About 76 percent of Francophones living outside Quebec live in Ontario and New Brunswick. Manitoba, Alberta and British Columbia each have approximately 50,000 Francophones, while Nova Scotia has 35,000 and Saskatchewan has fewer than 20,000. The areas with the smallest French-speaking populations are Prince Edward Island, Newfoundland and Labrador, and the three territories.

TIP ! For information on Francophone communities outside Quebec, visit the following Web sites: franco.ca/atlas/ or www.ocol-clo.gc.ca/7e_2.htm

History

Canada is a land of many cultures and many peoples. Aboriginal peoples have occupied the territory now called Canada for several thousands of years. Everybody else, either by birth or by descent, has been an immigrant -- we have all come from somewhere else. It has been said that Canada is a "nation of immigrants."

There are three main groups of Aboriginal peoples in Canada: the First Nations, the Inuit and the Métis. There are more than 50 different languages spoken by Canada's Aboriginal peoples, most of which are spoken only in Canada. In fact, the name "Canada" may have come from the word "Kanata," which means a settlement in the language of the Huron-Iroquois **First Nations peoples.**

As a country, Canada came into being on July 1, 1867. This event is known as "Confederation." Before 1867, the French arrived first, then the British. Each brought their own language, system of government, laws and culture. In 1763, after a long war between the British and the French, all of Canada came under British rule and was known as "British North America."

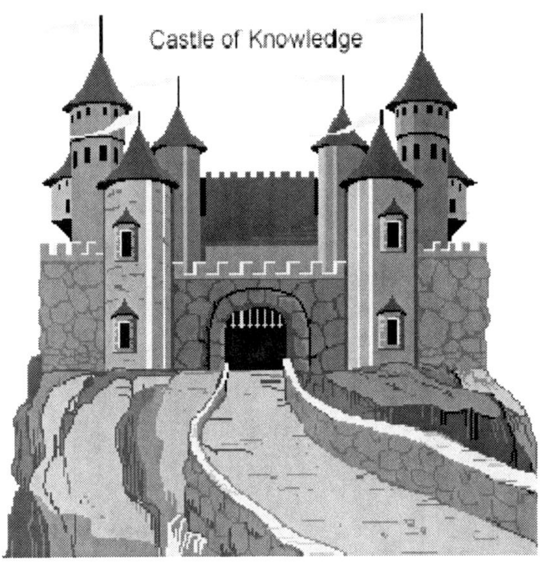

In the late 18th and into the 19th century, during and after the time of the American Revolution, many African-Americans and United

Empire Loyalists fled the United States for Canada, where British ties remained and slavery had been abolished.

During the mid- to late 19th and early 20th century, waves of immigrants arrived from Europe, attracted by the opportunity of a new and better life in Canada. Some settled in towns and cities; others worked in factories, mines and lumber camps. Many were farmers who turned the Prairie region into wheat fields. Asian immigrants from China, Japan and India settled mainly in the western provinces during this time. Many immigrants helped build Canada's national railways, which joined the east and west coasts and opened up the interior for settlement.

After both world wars, thousands of Europeans came to Canada as immigrants and refugees and helped build Canada's post-war economy. Canada's experience during and after the Second World War raised awareness of the needs of refugees and the desire of families to be together.

Over the last 50 years, people from all over the globe have sought a better life or have sought refuge in Canada, fleeing civil wars, political unrest and natural disasters.

Canada still needs the skills, talents and enthusiasm of newcomers to build our country, together with those who have come before them. All of this has been reflected in Canada's immigration and refugee policies. Today, Canada is home to immigrants from more than 240 countries. Most newcomers decide to become citizens of Canada, after they are settled and have met the requirements of Canadian citizenship.

Economy

Canada has a diversified economy. Natural resources industries, such as forestry, mining, oil and gas extraction, farming and fishing, are important sources of jobs and export earnings. Canada is also a world leader in the fields of telecommunications, biotechnology, aerospace technologies and pharmaceuticals. More and more jobs involve work in service industries or in information technology. Along with the United States and Mexico, Canada is a partner in the North American Free Trade Agreement.

Canada has a decimal system of currency. The Canadian dollar is the basic unit of money. The most common paper bills are the $5, $10 and $20, but $50 and $100 bills are also used. Canadian coins include the penny (one cent), nickel (five cents), dime (10 cents), quarter (25 cents), loonie ($1) and toonie ($2).

Government

Canada is a federation, with a parliamentary system of government. Being a federation means that powers and responsibilities are divided between the federal government and the 10 provincial governments. Canada also has three territorial jurisdictions. Canada has three levels of government: federal, provincial and municipal (cities and towns). These governments are elected by the citizens of Canada.

Federal government (Government of Canada)

The federal government is responsible for:

- defence;
- foreign policy and foreign relations;
- banking;
- the postal service;
- criminal law;
- immigration; and
- citizenship.

Provincial governments

Provincial governments are responsible for:

- education; and
- municipal institutions.

They also share responsibility with the federal government for:

- health services;
- farming;
- social assistance;
- transportation; and
- the environment.

Territorial Governments

The Northwest Territories, Yukon and Nunavut are not sovereign units. They get their powers from the federal parliament, but they have elected assemblies that follow many of the same practices as the provincial governments.

Municipal Governments

Municipal governments have functions delegated to them by other levels of government. They are responsible for local matters and services. These include:

- police and fire protection;
- water and sewer services;
- recreation; and
- local public transportation.

If you are interested, the Web site canada.gc.ca/howgoc/glance_e.html has more information about how Canadians govern themselves.

Bilingualism

Under the *Official Languages Act,* Canada is an officially bilingual country. This means that Canadians have the right to get federal government services in English or French, no matter what part of Canada they are living in.

New Brunswick is the only province that is officially bilingual. New Brunswick residents receive services in both official languages from all of their provincial government departments and agencies.

In Quebec, French is the official language and in most cases, provincial and municipal services are provided in French.

In the other provinces and territories, English is the official language, and the availability of provincial services in both official languages varies.

At the municipal level, the availability of services in both official languages varies greatly.

Multiculturalism

Canada is populated by people who have come from every part of the world. Through the *Canadian Multiculturalism Act,* the government encourages Canadians to take pride in their language, religion and heritage and to keep their customs and traditions, as long as they don't break Canadian laws.

Protecting the environment --Sustainable development

Canada has a beautiful natural environment. Because we have lots of land and a small population, most of our country is wild and unspoiled. However, it is becoming harder to preserve our environment as our population and cities grow. Pollution helps cause large-scale environmental problems, such as acid rain. And as more people use and live in natural areas, threats to the environment increase.

Canadians are very concerned about environmental issues. They know that damage to the environment can be hard to fix.

Canadians know that economic growth is crucial for the future prosperity of Canada. But growth must be managed carefully so that it does not harm the environment. The Canadian government is committed to "sustainable development," which is economic growth that does not hurt the environment and helps people.

A healthy environment is important to quality of life. Everyone living in Canada should act in a responsible way, both toward the environment and within their community. This way, future Canadians have the opportunity to live in a country that is clean and prosperous. Both individuals and groups can help Canada develop in a sustainable way.

Here are a few things you can do to help protect quality of life:

- throw waste paper and other garbage in public garbage cans;
- compost, recycle and re-use as many products as possible, such as paper, glass and cans;
- conserve energy and water by turning off lights and taps when you are not using them;
- walk, join a car pool, or use a bicycle or public transit whenever possible;
- use products that are environmentally friendly;
- plant trees or grow a garden, but avoid using chemicals;
- never pour paint, oil or other harmful chemicals down sinks or toilets, into sewers or onto the ground (telephone your local government to find out where you can throw out these hazardous materials);
- volunteer with a local organization; and
- educate yourself and your children about environmental issues.

For further information, contact:

Environment Canada
Enquiry Centre
351 St. Joseph Boulevard
Hull, Quebec K1A 0H3

Telephone: 1 (819) 997-2800
1 800 668-6767 (toll-free, within Canada)

Fax: 1 (819) 953-2225

E-mail: enviroinfo@ec.gc.ca
Web site: www.ec.gc.ca

TIP ! Contact your local government to find out about the services and bylaws that protect the environment (for example, garbage disposal schedules, water management and recycling programs). You can find local government telephone numbers in the Blue Pages of the telephone book.

Chapter 17

THE CANADIAN WAY OF LIFE

- **Family life and family law**
- **Marriage, divorce and the law**
- **Birth control and family planning**
- **Youth and their parents**
- **Youth and the law**
- **Standards and expectations**
- **Important social standards**
- **Some Canadian laws**
- **Interacting with officials**
- **People in authority**
- **Public officials**
- **Police officers**

Family Life And Family Law

Many people in Canada find that it takes two incomes to raise a family, even though parents are having fewer children. Most mothers have a job outside the home, and in many families, both parents share the work of shopping, cooking, cleaning the house and looking after the children. Because divorce has become more common, there are many one-parent families in Canada. Most single parents who raise their children on a full-time basis are women. There are also same-sex couples with children.

Marriage, divorce and the law

Canadian law views marriage as a legal agreement or contract between a man and a woman. Married people are considered equal partners. Marriage laws apply to all Canadian citizens and permanent residents. Many unmarried couples live together. In most provinces, unmarried heterosexual couples who have lived together for a certain period of time have legal status as "common-law" couples. They may call each other "husband" and "wife," or they may simply say "my partner."

Either the wife or the husband can ask for a divorce. This request will normally be approved by the courts if both people have agreed to end the marriage. Divorce will also be approved if one partner has been harmed through cruelty, adultery or a similar injustice.

Birth control and family planning

Many people use birth control. It is a matter of personal choice. Women can get a prescription for birth control pills from a doctor. Family planning information is available from government departments of health and public health offices, as well as from local health clinics. Abortion is legal but is only available from a doctor.

Youth and their parents

When children arrive in Canada, they usually learn about Canadian life quickly through schools, television, movies and music. If they need to learn English or French, they often learn it quite quickly.

Parents find out about Canadian life differently, as they search for housing and work. They too may need to learn English or French, but often need more time than their children to do so.

If you have children, you will know that you see the world somewhat differently than they do, because you are older and have more life experience. After immigrating to Canada, however, you may find that these differences increase, because you are having

different experiences of Canadian life. These differences affect the behaviour of all family members and can lead to tension in the family between parents and their children.

Discussing concerns with teachers, doctors, public health workers, social workers, settlement workers, and friends and relatives who have already settled in Canada will help you and your children understand your experiences and make good choices about your future.

Youth and the law

Youth in Canada who commit a crime are held accountable for their actions. However they are not dealt with in the same way as adult offenders. This is because they may not have an adult's understanding of their crime. They are also more likely than adult offenders to be reformed and become law-abiding citizens. The law for young offenders is called the *Youth Criminal Justice Act.*

Sweetheart ! I'm your new secretary and here is the key for your next business office in Canada.

Chapter 18

STANDARDS AND EXPECTATIONS

Some of Canada's standards for public behaviour may be more conservative than you are used to, while others may seem more liberal. For example, Canadians may seem impersonal and cold to some newcomers; to others, we may seem overly friendly.

Important social standards

Social practices -- not laws -- govern many types of behaviour in Canada. Some traditions are well established and are politely but firmly enforced. For example:

- **Lining up, or queuing:** People normally line up or queue according to the principle of "first-come, first-served." They will be angry if you push ahead in a line-up instead of waiting your turn.
- **Not smoking in private homes:** Most Canadians do not smoke. When you are in people's homes, you should always ask their permission to smoke. If they do not smoke themselves, they may ask you to go outside to smoke.
- **Being on time:** You should always arrive on time -- at school, at work and for any meeting. People who are often late may be fired from their jobs or suspended from school. Many Canadians will not wait more than 10 or 15 minutes for someone who has a business meeting. For social events, people expect that you will arrive within half an hour of the stated time.
- **Respect for the environment:** Canadians respect the natural environment and expect people to avoid littering (dropping waste paper and other garbage on the street or throwing it out of your car). They will expect you to carry your garbage until you can find a proper garbage can.

- **Bargaining:** Bargaining for a better price is not common in Canada, but there are some exceptions. For example, almost everyone bargains for a better price when buying a car or a house, or other expensive items such as furniture. People who sell things privately may also bargain.
- **Smart shopping:** Stores compete with one another to attract customers, so it is wise to check and compare prices at different stores before you buy.
- **Note:** The price marked on goods in stores does not usually include the federal and provincial sales taxes, which add from 7 percent to 15 percent to the cost of an item, depending on the province in which you buy it.

TIP ! If you have questions about social standards or customs, you can ask the local immigrant-serving organization for advice. If you have been matched with a Canadian family under the Host Program, the family members can help answer your questions as well.

SOME CANADIAN LAWS

Some laws you should be aware of

- It is illegal to drive without a driver's licence, registration and insurance.
- It is illegal to drive if you have been drinking alcohol.
- The driver and all passengers must wear seat belts at all times when driving in Canada.
- Babies and children who are too small to wear seat belts must be placed in properly installed infant or child car seats, appropriate to the age and weight of the child.
- Children under 12 years of age cannot be left at home alone, or to care for younger children.
- All children aged six to 16 must attend school.
- Smoking is not permitted in federal buildings, in elevators, on Canadian airlines, on buses and on other public transportation, nor in many banks, shops, restaurants and other public places (some municipalities have banned smoking in all public buildings).
- Depending on which part of Canada you live in, you must be either 18 or 19 years old to buy or drink alcohol in any form.
- It is against the law to hit your spouse or children, either in the home or in public.
- It is illegal to use, buy or sell marijuana, heroin, cocaine and other addictive drugs.

- It is illegal to make any kind of sexual remarks or advances if the other person does not like them.

Interacting With Officials

Knowing how to behave and what to expect can be very useful when you are dealing with public officials and people in authority. Usually, there is no need to worry about making mistakes. Except for matters of law, most Canadians do not insist on strict formality. Officials who know that you are a newcomer will make allowances for your inexperience with Canadian ways.

People in authority

In Canada, a person's authority is related to his or her position and responsibility. Women hold the same kinds of positions as men and have the same kinds of authority. People do not have authority just because of their name, status, social class or sex.

Public officials

Public officials will normally treat you in a polite but impersonal way. Public officials follow set procedures. They do not make the rules. They may not want to or be able to become involved with your situation. Do not respond to them in a personal or emotional way. Never try to bribe a public official. Bribery and other forms of corruption are illegal and will offend most Canadians.

Police Officers

The police are part of the community and are accountable to the public. They may be either men or women. They are trained to serve and protect the public, including you. Police operate within strict regulations and follow established procedures. Canadians expect honesty and fairness from the police.

Calling the police: Most cities and towns have an emergency number for the police. Call this number if you or someone else is hurt or in danger, or if you see a crime taking place. In most parts of Canada, the emergency number is 911. Emergency numbers are always printed inside the front cover of the telephone book.

What if you are questioned by a police officer?

- Call the police officer "officer."
- Accept the police officer's authority; do not try to argue.
- Be ready to show identification if a police officer asks you for it. If you are stopped by the police while driving a car,

the officer will probably ask you for your driver's licence, proof of insurance and car registration.

- Tell the officer the facts about what has happened. Do not offer your own opinion.
- Never try to give money to a police officer. Canadians do not bribe police officers. It is a serious crime to do this.

What if you are arrested by a police officer?

- Police officers must tell you who they are and show you their badge number.
- They must explain why they are arresting you and tell you what your rights are.
- They must allow you to call a lawyer right away. If you don't have a lawyer, they must give you the Legal Aid telephone number and let you call.
- You do not have to give any information, other than your name and address, until you have talked to a lawyer.

Chapter 19

YOUR RIGHTS AND OBLIGATIONS

- **Personal rights and freedoms**
- **Children's rights**
- **Women's rights**
- **Senior citizens' rights**
- **Becoming a Canadian citizen**
- **Responsible and active citizenship**

As a newcomer, you should be aware of your rights and obligations. Having the right to participate in Canadian society also means that you have a responsibility to respect the rights and freedoms of others and to obey Canada's laws.

Personal rights and freedoms

The *Canadian Charter of Rights and Freedoms* describes the basic principles and values by which Canadians live. The Charter is part of Canada's Constitution. The Charter protects you from the moment you arrive on Canadian soil. It gives everyone in Canada the following fundamental rights and freedoms:

- the right to life, liberty and personal security;
- freedom of conscience and religion;
- freedom of thought, belief, opinion and expression, including freedom of the press and other media of communication;
- freedom to hold peaceful meetings;
- freedom to join groups;
- the right to live and work anywhere in Canada;
- protection from unreasonable search or seizure and arbitrary detainment and imprisonment;
- the right to be presumed innocent until proven guilty;
- the right to have a lawyer;
- the right to a fair trial, through due process of law; and
- the right to equal protection and benefit under the law, without discrimination.

Children's Rights

In Canada, you are required by law to properly care for your children. Police, doctors, teachers and children's aid officials will act when children are being abused. This includes any form of harm and abuse -- physical, psychological or sexual. All forms of child abuse are serious crimes. In serious cases of abuse, children can be taken away from their parents.

Physical abuse is any intentional physical contact that causes injury. For example, spanking a child long enough or hard enough to cause bruises, or spanking with anything other than an open hand, is a form of abuse. Some cultural practices, such as female circumcision, are also considered physical abuse and are against the law.

Psychological abuse includes terror and humiliation.

Sexual abuse includes any form of sexual contact between an adult and a child.

Neglect is also a form of child abuse. Parents who fail to protect and provide for their children are guilty of neglect. By law, children **under 12 cannot be left alone to look after themselves or younger siblings.**

Kids' "help-lines" are available for children who need someone to help them or just need someone to talk to.

Women's rights

In Canada, women have the same legal status, rights and opportunities as men. Most Canadian men respect women as equals -- socially, in the workplace and in the home. Violence against women is against the law. Women who are abused can seek help for themselves and their children in local shelters. They are also entitled to legal protection to keep them safe.

Senior citizens' rights

A senior citizen is someone 65 years of age or older. It is common in Canadian society for healthy senior citizens to live on their own, instead of living with their children. Older people who need special care often move to a retirement or nursing home that provides trained staff and health-care workers. However, many Canadians still care for older family members in their own home.

Old Age Security: The Old Age Security (OAS) program ensures a basic income to all people in Canada 65 years of age or over who meet the residence requirements. Usually, OAS is paid after a person has lived in Canada at least 10 years, although people who have lived or worked in countries with which Canada has an agreement may qualify after as little as one year. Low-income people who get OAS may also qualify for the Guaranteed Income Supplement (GIS) and their spouses (or widows) may also qualify for the Spouse's Allowance if they are between 60 and 64 years of age.

The Canada Pension Plan pays benefits to contributors in the event of retirement or disability, as well as benefits to surviving spouses and orphans in the event of death of a contributor. All workers in Canada contribute to the plan.

> **TIP !** You may also be eligible for old age security benefits from your former country.

Guess who is she?
Clue: Ask anybody from India

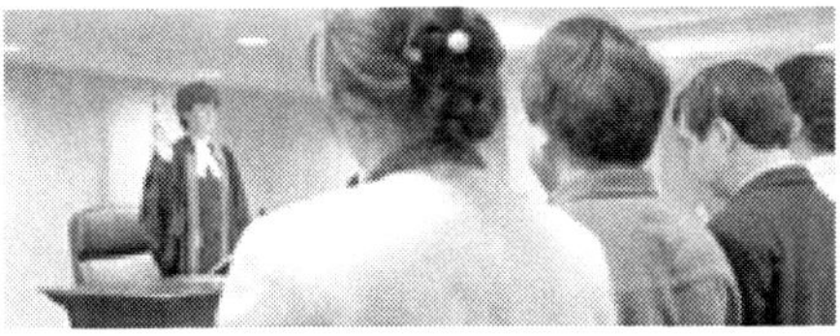

Becoming A Canadian Citizen

Once you have been in Canada for at least three years, you may apply to become a Canadian citizen. Immigrants who become citizens have the same rights as citizens who were born in Canada. As a citizen you can:

- vote and be a candidate for political office in federal, provincial and territorial elections;
- apply for a Canadian passport;
- enter and leave Canada freely;
- enjoy full economic rights, including the right to own any type of property; and
- be eligible for some pension benefits.

An adult applying for Canadian citizenship must:

- be at least 18 years old;
- be a permanent resident of Canada who entered the country legally;
- have lived in Canada for three of the four years before applying for citizenship;
- speak either English or French;
- know something about Canada's history, geography, system of government and voting;
- know the rights and responsibilities of citizenship;
- apply for citizenship and pass the citizenship test; and

- take the oath of citizenship.

You cannot become a Canadian citizen if you:

- are considered a risk to Canada's security;
- are under a deportation order;
- are in prison, on parole from prison or on probation; or
- have been found guilty of a serious crime within the past three years.

Responsible and active citizenship

For many Canadians, being a good citizen means getting involved in their community. Regardless of your interests, contributing to your society is rewarding and is appreciated by others who, like you, are proud to make Canada their home.

> **TIP !** Getting involved in volunteer activities is also an excellent way to meet new people, make friends, practise English or French, and learn about Canadian customs.

AFTERWORD

We hope this information has answered some of your questions about Canada, about adapting to life in Canada and about the Canadian way of life. As you prepare to leave for Canada, refer again to the tips and checklists provided here.

One last checklist:

- Have you gathered all of your essential and important documents? Have you had them translated into English or French?
- Have you considered buying health insurance for the time you are traveling and for the short period before you become eligible for Canada's Medicare system?
- Do you know what you can and cannot bring into Canada?
- Have you prepared yourself for finding work in Canada?
- Have you researched Canada's labour market in general and in each of the five regions? Have you used the Internet to learn about finding work in Canada?
- Have you considered living in one of Canada's smaller or medium-sized cities, or in a rural community? Have you used the Internet to learn about these choices?
- Have you considered the season and climate you will find when you arrive, and the clothing that you will need?
- Have you considered contacting an immigrant-serving organization soon after you arrive in Canada?
- Have you considered taking English or French lessons through the LINC (Language Instruction for Newcomers to Canada) program?

The best way to adjust to your new home will be to get involved! Try to speak English or French as much as possible, even if you make mistakes. Ask questions when you need help. Most people are pleased to help and will understand your needs. With time, you will feel more and more at home. Canada and Canadians will welcome you and your family into the larger Canadian family. Good luck on your journey!

Welcome to Canada -- your new home

Let me cool down a bit before leaving for Canada –its hot here in Arizona

We Canadians, welcome Americans

Feel free to call us, you are welcome anytime

I can teach you , how to live around ice and snow

Montreal Casino

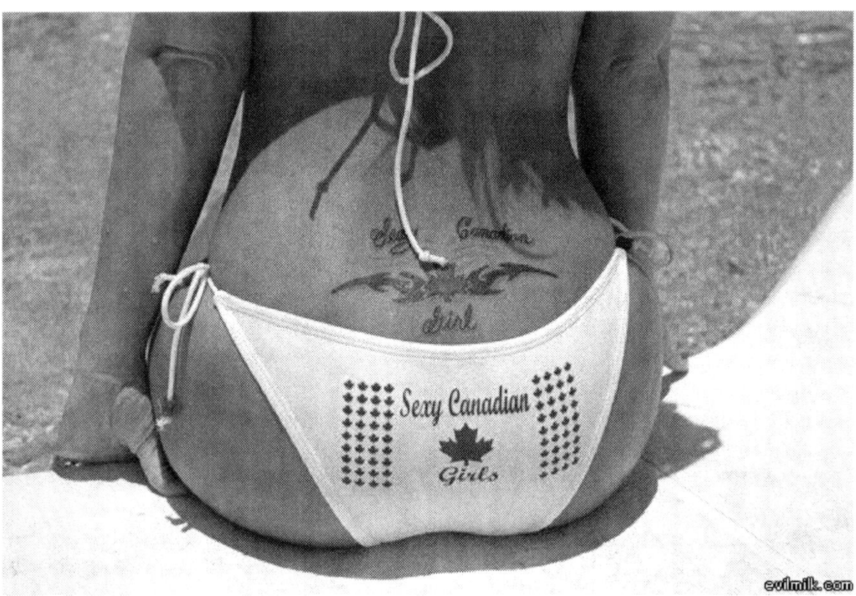

Vancouver

Toronto

CANADA

Tonight my hockey team is not doing well

Leasfs show me your talent, otherwise!

TORONTO
MAPLE
LEAFS
®

TORONTO
RAPTORS

RUGBY
CANADA

My job is to melt the ice Eh!

NIAGARA FALLS

Wanna play hockey? Eh!

Where's do I vote?

INDEX

Printed in the United States
206304BV00001B/12/P

9 780980 920345